The EB-5 Handbook

A Guide for Investors and Developers

JEFF CAMPION

LINDA HE (何梅)

DAVID HIRSON

ALI JAHANGIRI

LINDA LAU

DAWN LURIE

JOSEPH MCCARTHY

ELIZABETH PENG

AL RATTAN

REID THOMAS

JOHN TISHLER

KYLE WALKER

CLETUS WEBER

KEVIN WRIGHT

EB5Investors.com books may be purchased for educational, business, or sales promotional use. For information, please e-mail info@eb5investors.com. Domestic in United States please call 1 (800) 997 1228 (United States). For international assistance, please call

+1 (949) 271-9030.

For corrections, updates, comments, or any other inquiries please e-mail info@eb5investors.com.

First Printing, 2014

ISBN: 0991564820

ISBN-13: 978-0-9915648-2-8

TABLE OF CONTENTS

Published By
EB5investors.com
&
EB5 Investors Magazine

PREFACE
By Ali Jahangiri

The EB-5 industry is frequently misrepresented; there is rhetoric like "foreign nationals are buying green cards," "operatives are exploiting the program to threaten national security," and "it's just a scam." However, having personally spoken with EB-5 investors and project developers who have achieved success through the program, I know this simply isn't true. One example that sticks out in my mind is the case of an immigrant investor I met in early 2014. This man was in his early 30s and he came to my office with his sister, who was 22 years old. He was a savvy businessman who started from nothing and built up a trading company between his home country and Russia. He did all of this not for himself, but for his sister, who needed residency in the United States to further her education at UCLA. This case is not out of the ordinary—many of the investors I speak with are self-made and have worked tremendously hard for their success, and many use this money to fund immigration for the future of their families. Their stories are more important and a better window into the program than uninformed rabble-rousing and sensationalism.

While not as detrimental as having a misinformed opinion about EB-5, many people have no knowledge of EB-5 whatsoever. So what are the bare bones facts of the EB-5 program? What exactly do EB-5 immigrant investors sign up for? It certainly isn't as simple as "buying" a green card, and US job creation is at the heart of the program. Applicants must invest at least $500,000 in a US company and create 10 jobs for US workers with that capital. The process isn't easy, but the program is a win-win-win situation for immigrant investors, business owners and project developers, and the US economy. For immigrant investors, a successful EB-5 application means a green card and permanent residency in the United States. For business owners and project developers, an EB-5 investment means low-cost capital to create, develop, and even save businesses and projects. For the US economy, the EB-5 program means an influx of spending, job creation, and tax revenue, which all equal economic growth. With all of these benefits going for the EB-5 program, why does it remain so obscure and inaccessible?

I had these very same sorts of questions and wasn't always an expert in EB-5. When I first learned of the program, its advantages immediately compelled me. The program also interested me on a personal level, as the child of immigrant parents, a former securities lawyer, and the founder of my own business. Unfortunately, the vast majority of the material written on EB-5 topics was, and still is, obscure and heavy in legal jargon. Even with my background in law and my interest in learning more about the program, I almost quit before ever starting my EB-5 journey. The many benefits of the program were often overshadowed by inaccessible, intimidating, and unapproachable language. However, instead of giving up, I decided to make a change in EB-5 media and promote simplicity, accessibility, and transparency.

This goal has led to the creation of impressive EB-5 resources. My company publishes EB5 Investors Magazine, which features articles from respected EB-5 professionals and in-house analysis of key issues. We also manage EB5Investors.com, a series of international websites dedicated to providing useful and accessible information about the EB-5 program. People interested in EB-5 ask us every day for clarity on topics from basic visa requirements to what makes an EB-5 project compliant. The sheer number of questions we receive illuminates the lack of accessible, easy-to-understand information in a program with growing popularity.

This is where *The EB-5 Handbook* comes in. This book acts as an entry point, both for the immigrant investor who has never heard of the program, and for the sophisticated business person who has specific questions about EB-5 in the capital stack. Unlike other resources written by a single individual, this handbook has aggregated an impressive team of EB-5 practitioners writing about their own expertise. With immigration attorneys, regional center owners, project developers, a securities attorney, an economist, a migration agency and the executive of an escrow company on board, *The EB-5 Handbook* sets itself apart in quality and diversity of information. To give you a full picture of the breadth of their experience, I have included the authors' biographies. I am truly lucky to be working with these experienced authors and our talented editorial team.

HOW TO USE THIS BOOK

The unique authorship of *The EB-5 Handbook* has also led to a unique structure for the reader. With so much know-how on board, this book provides information tailored to both the immigrant investor and the project developer.

In order to meet these two distinct goals, the book is divided into two parts, and written for two distinct audiences:

Part I—For the Investor

Foreign investors should know what to expect when they participate in the EB-5 visa program. Part I of this book explains the program in simple terms, makes the program easy to learn, and gives investors the information they need to get started. This part also walks readers through the basics of the program, as well as how to find EB-5 projects, how to conduct due diligence, and how to apply for a green card. After reading Part I, investors will be able to confidently assemble their team of EB-5 professionals, invest in a US project and start the process of receiving their green cards.

Part II—For the Developer

Part II focuses on the developer's goals. Developers should know if their project is a good fit for EB-5 before they consider raising EB-5 capital. If developers do not take the time to weigh their options and plan accordingly, they may fail to raise any EB-5 capital after paying substantial up-front costs. Part II of this book will help developers identify if EB-5 capital is right for them, learn how to market projects to EB-5 investors, understand how EB-5 can be utilized in the capital stack, contemplate regional center options, raise capital for their projects, and know their responsibilities following the capital raise. After reading Part II, developers can assess the desirability and practicality of EB-5 for their projects and have some basic tools to begin their EB-5 journey.

PUBLISHER, AUTHORS, AND EDITORS

THE PUBLISHER

Ali Jahangiri

Ali Jahangiri is the CEO of EB5Investors.com and EB5 Investors Magazine, the EB-5 industry's leading trade publication and online portal. EB5Investors.com offers a unique online platform, allowing investors to communicate directly with immigration attorneys, and developers to connect with EB-5 regional centers and funding sources. EB5 Investors Magazine proudly hosts two of the trade's largest conferences each year in the United States. Ali holds a Juris Doctor from Loyola Marymount University and his Bachelors of Science from University of California, Irvine. He began his career practicing corporate securities law, but shifted his focus to digital publishing, where he pioneered multiple digital interactive portals. Ali was appointed in 2009 and 2010 by then-Gov. Arnold Schwarzenegger to the Law Revision Commission and OC Fair Board, respectively.

THE AUTHOR TEAM

Jeff Campion

Jeff Campion is an immigration lawyer and the CEO of Pathways EB-5, Texas Urban Triangle Regional Center, and Gulf States Regional Center, which own and operate regional centers covering multiple states. Jeff earned his Juris Doctor from Florida's Levin College of Law and his Master's in Latin American Studies from the University of Florida. He is a member of the AILA EB-5 Committee, a board member of the AILA Mexico Chapter, and serves as an IIUSA Public Policy Committee member. Jeff provides services for investors and project developers and specializes in the formation of regional centers, project compliance, immigration risk assessment, and regional center oversight. He frequently lectures and speaks on panels involving the EB-5 industry.

Linda He (何梅)

Linda He is the president of Wailian Overseas Consulting Group, among the largest immigration agencies in China, with more than 300 employees, and offices spread across all the first and second tier cities in China. Over the years, Wailian has enjoyed many success stories across more than 50 EB-5 projects. In 2013, Wailian raised approximately $250 million and created more than 5,000 jobs for the New York region alone. Wailian also proudly hosts China's largest annual EB-5 conference, with the purpose of building a valuable communication platform for developers, regional centers, immigration agents, and investors. Linda is also active in the community and she is an avid philanthropist who serves as the vice chairman of the Chinese American Association and director of the Shanghai Soong Ching Ling - Pearl S. Buck Foundation.

David Hirson

David Hirson is the managing partner of David Hirson & Partners, LLP. Prior to opening his own firm, he was the co-managing partner of the Irvine, California office of Fragomen, Del Rey, Bernsen & Loewy, LLP. David graduated from the University of the Witwatersrand in Johannesburg, South Africa, and is a member of both the California and Washington, D.C. bars. He has been involved with the EB-5 program since its inception in 1990 and successfully filed one of the program's first cases. David has served as the chairman of the State Bar of California, International Law Section and chairman of the American Immigration Lawyers Association (AILA), Southern California Chapter. Among a list of notable mentions, David has been recognized as a Southern California Super Lawyer. His law practice focuses on EB-5 regional centers, projects, and direct and regional center individual investors. David frequently lectures domestically and abroad on the topic of EB-5 and immigration law, and serves on the editorial board of EB5 Investors Magazine.

Linda Lau

Linda Lau is the founder of Global Law Group, which specializes in immigration cases involving high net-worth individuals and foreign companies. Linda has served as the chair of the Southern California chapter of the American Immigration Lawyers Association (AILA). She is a member of the California State Bar and is admitted as a solicitor of England and Wales. She frequently speaks on EB-5 matters at conferences and seminars. Linda earned her Juris Doctor from the University of California, Los Angeles, her master's from the University of Michigan and her bachelor's degree from the University of California, Berkeley. Linda is a member of the editorial board of EB5 Investors Magazine.

Dawn Lurie

Dawn Lurie is an EB-5 immigration attorney based in Washington, D.C., at Polsinelli. She earned her Bachelor of Arts from Pennsylvania State University and her Juris Doctor from American University's Washington College of Law. Dawn has been admitted to the bar in both New Jersey and Washington, D.C., and has been involved in EB-5 matters since the early 1990s. Dawn is a member of IIUSA's Best Practice Committee. A specialist in EB-5 compliance matters, she has represented EB-5 regional centers at EB-5 board hearings before the EB-5 office in Washington, D.C., dealing with exemplar and I-829-related issues.

Joseph McCarthy

Joseph McCarthy is a co-founder of American Dream Fund, an operator of multiple nationwide EB-5 regional centers, and a partner with the Los Angeles-based firm McAdam & McCarthy. He earned his Juris Doctor from Seattle University School of Law, his Master of Science in Hydrogeology and Aqueous Geochemistry from the Colorado School of Mines and his Bachelor of Arts in Geology from Whittier

College. Through the American Dream Fund, Joseph has raised more than $350 million for EB-5 real estate projects. He is a member of the American Immigration Lawyers Association and serves on the editorial board for EB5 Investors Magazine.

Al Rattan

Al Rattan is a developer and EB-5 regional center owner. He received his Bachelor of Science in Business Administration from Sacramento State University and has more than 30 years of hands-on real estate development experience. He specializes in the construction and development of new residential communities, industrial buildings, retail shopping centers, office buildings, acute care medical centers, and senior care retirement communities. Al is the co-founder and president of an Asian investment opportunity fund known as Continental East Development (CED), which is headquartered in Murrieta, California. Currently, CED, in partnership with USA Continental Regional Center, is actively pursuing the development of senior assisted living, memory care, and skilled nursing communities through the EB-5 visa program.

Reid Thomas

Responsible for global sales and marketing at NES Financial, Reid brings over 20 years of sales and marketing leadership in both public and private companies in high-growth Silicon Valley technology companies. His past experience includes leading sales with Voice Over IP pioneer Sylantro Systems, driving revenue and market share growth to a successful IPO with VINA Technologies, and running sales operations at Octel Communications, which was acquired by Lucent Technologies. Prior to his current position, Reid served as SVP of Global Sales at Laszlo Systems, a global leader and pioneer in Rich Internet Applications. During his time with NES Financial, Reid has been instrumental in the rapid growth of the company's EB-5 business, making NES Financial the leader in EB-5 by providing innovative solutions specifically built for the industry. His active participation in the EB-5 community has made him a frequent and sought after speaker at events and conferences across the country.

John Tishler

John Tishler is a partner at Sheppard Mullin Richter & Hampton, LLP, where he currently serves as co-chair of the firm's capital markets practice team and chair of the firm's EB-5 practice team. He regularly advises clients on domestic and international capital markets, corporate finance, investment vehicle structuring, business transactions and mergers and acquisitions. John's EB-5 clients include developers, regional centers and intermediaries. He also advises established NYSE, NASDAQ and international exchange issuers and smaller high-growth clients on capital structures, equity and debt offerings, and securities law compliance. John received his Juris Doctor from Yale Law School and his Bachelor of Arts in Economics from Cornell University. He frequently writes on EB-5 capital markets and speaks on EB-5 securities-related panels.

Kyle Walker

Kyle Walker is co-founder of Green Card Fund Regional Center and a managing partner of newGen Worldwide, an international real estate firm specializing in capital formation, development, holdings, and brokerage. He attended Arizona State University, where he earned his Bachelor of Science in Interdisciplinary Studies with a focus in business, urban planning, and sustainability. He has raised more than $85 million for EB-5 real estate projects with a 100 percent success rate of I-526 approvals. He is also a member of the Greater Phoenix Economic Council's (GPEC) International Leadership Council and is a founding member of the China Arizona Center. Kyle also serves as chairman of the IIUSA membership committee.

Kevin Wright

Kevin Wright serves as economist and CEO of Wright Johnson, LLC. He has assisted over 70 business enterprises to become USCIS-designated EB-5 regional centers, and has also worked on numerous successful direct EB-5 projects. Wright Johnson, LLC prepares economic impact studies and supporting business plans for USCIS submittal. Kevin has completed such studies and business plans for numerous industries, including hospitality, hospitals, oil and gas, farming, assisted living and nursing care, and technology. He lectures frequently on EB-5 economic matters and is a committee member for IIUSA.

THE EDITORIAL TEAM

Cletus Weber, Editor-in-Chief

Cletus M. Weber is a co-founder of Peng & Weber, PLLC, a nationally recognized EB-5 immigration law firm based in Seattle/Mercer Island, Washington. He serves on the national EB-5 Committee of the American Immigration Lawyers Association (AILA) and is a frequent speaker and experienced author and editor on EB-5 law and practice. Cletus is associate editor of AILA's 2010 and 2014 books on EB-5, and invited reviewer of the EB-5 section of *Kurzban's Immigration Law Sourcebook,* the "bible" on American immigration law. Cletus earned his bachelor's degree from the College of William and Mary and his Juris Doctor from the George Washington University Law School.

Elizabeth Peng, Editor-in-Chief (Chinese Version)

Elizabeth Peng is co-founder of Peng & Weber, PLLC, a nationally- recognized EB-5 immigration law firm based in Seattle/Mercer Island, Washington. Elizabeth earned law degrees in both China (1983) and the United States (1988). Elizabeth is a respected author and lecturer on EB-5, especially with respect to EB-5 investors from China. Among other articles, she has written "How to Successfully Represent Chinese Investors in EB-5" for *The EB-5 Book* (2012) and "Insiders' Guide to EB-5 Immigrant Investor Law and Practice" for *Immigration Options for Investors & Entrepreneurs*, 3rd Edition.

Courtney Creedon, Editor

Courtney Creedon is the editor of EB5 Investors Magazine, headquartered in Irvine, California. She received her Bachelors of Science in Foreign Service from the Edmund A. Walsh School of Foreign Service at Georgetown University in Washington, D.C., where she focused on international immigration issues. She has worked with immigrant and refugee communities in Washington, D.C.; Copenhagen, Denmark; and Orange County, California.

Ali Jahangiri, Editor; John Tishler, Editor; Leah Quillian, Editor; Hannah Huff, Assistant Editor; Nicole Connolly, Assistant Editor

PART I

Guide for the Investor

INTRODUCTION
By Kevin Wright

The EB-5 visa program gives *you*, a foreign investor, the chance to obtain a green card by investing in a business in the United States. Even if you lack business experience, the program's requirements are relatively simple. As a foreign investor, you must:

- make an investment of $500,000[1] or $1 million, depending on where the business project is located in the United States
- create (or in very limited circumstances, preserve) 10 jobs for US workers through your investment

For many EB-5 investors, the primary goal of participating in the program is to get a US green card. Thousands of people with little to no business experience have been able to come to the United States through the program, so do not let the requirements of the program deter you. Of course, the process of making an investment and creating jobs does require a certain amount of preparation, but there is a dedicated network of EB-5 professionals in the United States—and abroad—who can guide you through the process. Because the EB-5 program is a mixture of business and immigration, it is important that you work with a team that understands all of the aspects of the EB-5 program, and this book will help you do just that.

If you are reading this book, you likely have already heard of EB-5, but there are a number of other visa options to consider—and not all programs offer green cards—so you may be asking yourself, *What is a green card? Is EB-5 right for me?* This book will help you answer these questions and will guide you throughout the EB-5 visa process.

LEGAL STATUS IN THE UNITED STATES

Immigrant Status. As you will discover, getting a green card through any visa program—not just EB-5—is a long but worthwhile process. Having a green card means that you have immigrant status in the United States. With immigrant status, the US government considers you a permanent resident of the United States. Being a permanent resident (that is, being a green card holder) is not the same thing as being a citizen, but permanent residency and citizenship share

1.   Congress has for a number of years considered changes to various parts of the Immigration and Nationality Act (INA), which includes the EB-5 program, so it is possible that if and when Congress changes the INA, Congress may also include changes to these minimum investment amounts for the EB-5 program, resulting in an increase of the minimum investment.

many core elements. If you are a permanent resident, you can live and work anywhere in the United States, own property in the United States, attend US public schools, and join certain branches of the military. However, there are some rights, such as voting, that only US citizens have. This book will explain some of the major differences between permanent residency and citizenship.

Nonimmigrant Status. You should know that not all visa programs offer permanent residency. Some visas only let you live in the United States temporarily. The amount of time that nonimmigrants (that is, foreigners who are legally but temporarily living in the United States) can stay in the United States depends on their particular visa. While green card holders are able to permanently live in the United States, nonimmigrants can only temporarily live in the United States for specific purposes, such as for business or pleasure, academic study, temporary employment, or other specified purposes. (**Note:** If you enter the United States *illegally*, you have neither immigrant status nor nonimmigrant status. As an illegal immigrant, you normally are ineligible to participate in EB-5.)

Table A breaks down common visas you may have heard of into two categories: visas that grant immigrant status (visas that give you green cards) and visas that grant nonimmigrant status (visas that are only temporary).

Table A

Visas with Immigrant Status		
Visa Type	**Specific Visas Available**	**Approximate Number of Visas Granted Annually**
Family-Based Visas	**IR-1** (spouse of a US citizen) **IR-2** (unmarried child of a US citizen under 21) **IR-3** (orphan adopted abroad by a US citizen) **IR-4** (orphan adopted in the United States by a US citizen) **IR-5** (parent of a US citizen) **Family F1** (unmarried sons and daughters of US citizens and their minor children) **Family F2** (spouses, unmarried sons and daughters of legal permanent residents and their minor children) **Family F3** (married sons and daughters of US citizens and their minor children) **Family F4** (brothers and sisters of US citizens, their spouses, and minor children)	480,000 family-based visas are granted each year. *There is an unlimited number of visas granted to immediate relatives.*

Employment-Based Visas	**EB-1** (person with extraordinary ability, outstanding professors and researchers, multinational managers or executives) **EB-2** (professionals with an advanced degree, persons with exceptional ability) **EB-3** (skilled workers, professionals, unskilled/other workers) **EB-4** (special workers, including broadcasters, ministers, certain former employees, certain translators, and other specific employment) **EB-5** (immigrant investors like *you!*)	140,000 employment-based visas are granted each year. *The total number of visas available to EB-5 investors is 10,000.*
Diversity Visa (Lottery)	**DV** (randomly granted visas for foreign nationals in certain countries with low levels of US immigration)	55,000 diversity visas are granted each year.
Visas with Nonimmigrant Status	**E-1** (treaty traders) **E-2** (treaty investors) **H1-B** (person in specialty occupation) **H-2A** (temporary agricultural worker) **H-2B** (temporary non-agricultural worker) **H-3** (trainee or special education visitor) **K-1** (fiancé of US citizen) **L-1** (intracompany transferee) **O** (individual with extraordinary ability or achievement) **P-1** (individual or team athlete or member of an entertainment group) **P-2** and **P-3** (artist or entertainer) **Q-1** (participant in a cultural exchange program)	Some "H" visa categories have annual quotas; the other nonimmigrant visas do not have annual quotas.
Students	**F-1** (academic students) **M-1** (vocational students)	
Exchange Visitors	**J-1** (exchange visitors)	
Temporary Visitors for Pleasure	B-2 (visitors for pleasure) **Visa Waiver Program** (visitors from certain countries)	

As you can see from *Table A*, there are other visa options available for foreign investors, but many are based on existing connections to the United States—either through family or employment—and may not offer a permanent green card like the EB-5 visa does.

UNDERSTANDING THE EB-5 PROGRAM

The EB-5 program was introduced in 1990, with the hope of creating more jobs for US workers and boosting the US economy by raising money for development and employment. It stimulates the US economy with foreign investment and provides opportunity for immigrants.

As you read above, the EB-5 program requires you to make an investment of at least $1 million or at least $500,000, depending on the location of the project. To qualify for the lesser amount, you must invest in a project located in a targeted employment area, known as TEAs in the EB-5 industry. A TEA is a rural area or an area with high unemployment. The EB-5 program has this provision in order to help direct investment dollars to areas that need it the most. It also has the added benefit of allowing investors to qualify for the EB-5 program at a lesser amount. Economists that specialize in EB-5 work to identify these areas and have them certified with the appropriate government authorities. You do not need to know the intricacies of the process, but it is important to keep this term in mind, as it will come up when you are exploring investment opportunities.

There are two ways to invest your money through the EB-5 program. One method is referred to as "direct investment," and the other is referred to as "indirect investment" (or investing under a regional center). The direct option has stricter job requirements, while the indirect (regional center) option counts indirect and induced jobs. You will learn about both methods of investment in this book so that you know all of your options and can make an informed decision as to which option is right for you. Statistically, the regional center method (indirect) is the most popular among investors.

The Regional Center

So what exactly is a regional center? An EB-5 regional center is defined as a government approved entity, public or private, which is involved with the promotion of economic growth, improved regional productivity, job creation, and increased domestic capital investment. In practical terms, a regional center serves as an entity developers affiliate with in order to raise EB-5 capital. The regional center is like a license; the regional center designation allows projects to access EB-5 capital with specific job creation advantages.

The program says that your investment must create 10 jobs for US workers. If you invest under a regional center, you will be able to count multiple types of jobs towards that number. You, personally, will not be responsible for creating these jobs, but rather the money you have invested will allow a business to create the jobs, which means you will not have to open a business and hire workers yourself. But don't worry about that for now—as an investor, you will not be responsible for calculating how many jobs your investment has created. The team of EB-5 professionals you will learn about in Chapter 1 will be in charge of taking care of the details of your immigration process.

It is important to note that you are not investing *in* a regional center, but rather *under* a regional center. The regional center is involved with your investment, but your actual investment is directed to a project that you have chosen. Therefore, it is important to analyze the business or project itself, not just its affiliated regional center. Also, because the vast majority of investments in EB-5 (especially regional center cases) involve development or real estate projects, such as hotels, you may see both "project" and "business" used to describe the entity into which you make your EB-5 investment. The EB-5 professionals at regional centers are familiar with the steps of the EB-5 process and will be responsible for making sure that the project you are investing in is in compliance with all laws, along with preparing much of the paperwork you need to actually apply for the visa and permanent residency. An overwhelming majority of EB-5 investment is done under regional centers.

Direct Investment

For those investors who are interested in obtaining a green card and directly operating a business in the United States, the direct investment option may be a better choice. Direct investments have the same general requirements as regional center investments—invest at least $500,000 in a US business and create 10 US jobs—but it will be entirely up to you, the investor, to assemble your team of professionals and navigate the EB-5 process.

The most important difference between direct and indirect investments is *how* jobs are counted. If you make a direct investment, you can only count 10 jobs on the payroll. This means that if you open a flower shop, only the floral designers, cashiers, delivery persons, and other people employed directly by the flower shop can count as direct employees. These jobs are referred to as "direct jobs" under applicable EB-5 regulations.

Direct (Pooled or Syndicated) Investment

Although pooled or syndicated direct investments are not typical, it's good for you to know they exist in the market. This is where multiple EB-5 investors are combined for a direct investment rather than using a regional center. The obvious disadvantage for the project is job creation; not being able to count indirect and induced jobs. When we refer to direct investment in *The EB-5 Handbook*, we are not referring to this pooled or syndicated model. It's important for you to know that EB-5 direct investment projects are not reserved exclusively for single investor owner/operators looking to open a business in the United States and earn a green card. There is nothing in the regulations preventing the pooling of direct investments.

MAKING AN INVESTMENT

Whether you invest directly or under a regional center, finding a reputable project that is suitable to your immigration and investment needs is very important. Once you've found a project that you like, you will make your actual investment. To do this, you will most likely transfer your investment to an escrow account in the United States to begin the visa application process—although escrow is not required by EB-5 regulations, this is the most common way to commit your money to a project. Simply put, an escrow account is a third-party bank account that will hold onto your investment until the first form you file with the US government is approved. But this is not always the case. Sometimes, your money can be released to the project before this form is approved if those are the terms of the escrow agreement you sign with the regional center. The project's offering documents will describe the terms of the escrow agreement before you commit your money to a particular EB-5 project, so this will not be a surprise to you.

THE VISA APPLICATION PROCESS

Whether you choose a project yourself or an EB-5 professional recommends a particular project, your immigration attorney will assist you throughout the application process. To get a green card through the EB-5 program, you must:

1. File Form I-526 (Petition by Alien Entrepreneur). This form shows the US government that you have made an investment and it also explains how your investment is expected to create 10 jobs (you must also prove the "lawful" source of your investment funds at this time);

2. Obtain your "conditional" two-year green card. You do this either by: a) filing Form DS-260 at the National Visa Center (NVC) in the US. The NVC, after certain processing and the acceptance of processing fees, will send the case to a US consulate in your country of citizenship (a process called "consular processing"), which is normally the approach you would use if you are still living outside the United States at the time when you file for your "conditional" green card; or b) filing Form I-485 (Application to Register Permanent Status or Adjust Status), which is called "adjustment of status" (AOS). Adjustment of status is normally the approach you would use if you are already living in the United States in a nonimmigrant status, such as on a student visa or a work visa. Whichever path you use, you will then be able to begin living as a conditional permanent resident in the United States for two years while your investment dollars are creating jobs; and

3. File Form I-829 (Petition by Entrepreneur to Remove Conditions). At this stage, you normally need to prove you have sustained your investment throughout the two-year conditional residence period and have created the required number of jobs. This step is necessary to receive your permanent green card.

Your immigration attorney will file all necessary forms with United States Citizenship and Immigration Services (USCIS), the government agency in charge of the EB-5 program. Once you have made your investment, you can begin applying for the EB-5 visa by working with your immigration attorney. You will first file Form I-526 (Petition by Alien Entrepreneur). Your I-526 is the application used to show USCIS that you meet the qualifications to receive an EB-5 visa; namely, that you have made your investment and that the business plans to create 10 jobs with that investment. After your I-526 is approved by USCIS (and you have adjusted your status with Form I-485 or completed consular processing as described above), you, your spouse, and your unmarried children under the age of 21 will have a conditional residency in the United States.

During this two-year period, you will be a conditional permanent resident. This means that you can live and work in the United States and send your children to school. However, your stay in the United States during this time is conditional, so it is your responsibility to make sure you do not abandon your status as a resident or do anything that would jeopardize your stay. See Chapter 4 for more information about conditional permanent residency.

Near the end of the two-year conditional period, your immigration attorney will file Form I-829 with USCIS to prove how your investment has met the requirements of the EB-5 program. The I-829 typically shows that your investment has actually created 10 jobs (or is likely to do so within a reasonable time) and that all the other conditions of the program have been satisfied by the various players involved. If your attorney cannot show that jobs were created or are likely to be created within a reasonable time because of your investment, then you may not be able to get your green card. For this reason, it is important that you carefully select the project for your investment and hire an immigration attorney who is experienced in EB-5 in order to ensure that you understand what is required of you as an investor. This book will give you tips and help you navigate through the EB-5 process.

After your Form I-829 is approved by USCIS, you will be eligible to have your investment returned to you. How much if any is returned and when you will see your money again is determined in the project's exit strategy. The exit strategy is normally included in the project's paperwork when it comes time for you to commit to a particular project.

Don't worry too much about any forms or strategies for now—you will have the assistance of your immigration attorney and other EB-5 professionals to guide you through the immigration process.

HOW TO USE PART I—GUIDE FOR THE INVESTOR

Part I is an easy-to-use guide for you, the investor. It will help you navigate the EB-5 program, learn who the most important players are, and most importantly, become familiar with the visa application process so that you have a high probability of receiving your green card. After reading Part I, you will have all the necessary tools to hire the right professionals, choose a business to invest in, make your investment, and apply for your green card. The chapters in *The EB-5 Handbook* are put in the same order as your EB-5 process timeline so that you can get a firm understanding of EB-5 from beginning to end.

Chapter 1: Who Will I Meet?

To succeed in the EB-5 visa program, you will need assistance from certain experienced professionals. Chapter 1 will explain who these people are, what they do, and what to look for when choosing professionals to help you achieve your EB-5 goals. These important people include your migration agent (if applicable), your immigration attorney, the regional center, the project developer, and a few other important players who will work behind the scenes to help you succeed in the EB-5 visa program. It is important to have a working understanding of these people to fully grasp the EB-5 process and to feel more comfortable participating in the program.

Chapter 2: Where Do I Begin?

This chapter goes over the basics of what you will need to know to start your EB-5 journey. The first thing you will need to do is determine your eligibility for the EB-5 program and whether EB-5 is your best option for a green card. After determining if you are eligible for EB-5 and whether EB-5 is your best option, you will then decide whether you want to make a direct investment or an investment under a regional center. This chapter explains the differences between the two investment options and then discusses the ways you can find available EB-5 projects.

Chapter 3: Is This a Good Project?

Once you have identified a few projects that interest you, you will need to determine which one you will actually invest in. You will also review important business and legal issues with your chosen project—what people in the industry call "due diligence." When you conduct due diligence, you are attempting to get a solid understanding of the financial and immigration risks of the project. Chapter 3 also discusses the different outcomes that can result from project success or failure and the different ways projects can succeed and fail.

Chapter 4: How Do I Apply for My Visa?

As you will learn, you can normally become a temporary (i.e., "conditional") resident of the United States fairly quickly (usually within about two years), but becoming a permanent resident (i.e., without any conditions remaining) takes approximately four to five years to complete. This chapter will walk you through the steps you need to take in order to receive your green card. You will work with your immigration attorney and regional center (if applicable) to give USCIS all of the information, documents, and forms it needs to review you and your investment.

CHAPTER 1: WHO WILL I MEET?
By Jeff Campion

It takes a team of EB-5 experts to help you make a smart investment. As an EB-5 investor, you will interact with a number of individuals as you learn about the program, find a project, make your investment, and apply for your two-year "conditional" green card and, ultimately, your permanent green card. Each individual serves a different purpose, so understanding each player's role will be important to successfully obtaining your green card and getting the most out of your investment.

MIGRATION AGENT

Depending on which country you are from, a migration agent may be the first person you meet during the EB-5 process. Migration agents are immigration specialists who can help you find an EB-5 project, obtain and organize "source of funds" documentation you will need for governmental agencies in the United States, and introduce you to an immigration attorney. Most countries require migration agents to obtain a license. In China, migration agents have historically been the primary way for investors to locate quality EB-5 projects. These individuals normally work with many EB-5 investors and multiple projects and typically are familiar with the EB-5 process. Some migration agents will give you choices of which countries you can migrate to, including the United States. In EB-5, your migration agent will communicate directly with project developers and regional centers for you and may interpret between languages for you. Additionally, your migration agent will serve as your point of contact in your home country as you prepare to invest and immigrate.

If you know someone who has successfully migrated to the United States or other countries, this person can refer you to the migration agent or agency he or she used—or you can find agents through internet searches. Before hiring a migration agent, you should thoroughly research the agent (and/or agency). Like any other professional, migration agents work for a fee, and knowing how the migration agent works with other clients, such as regional centers and developers, will help you decide whether to hire the migration agent. Many migration agents will promote multiple EB-5 projects at once and will hold seminars in your home country that you can attend for specific information.

At these seminars, migration agents usually focus on a single EB-5 project, but they will normally know about many other available EB-5 projects they can connect you with. But remember, this agent may not prioritize you over other players—like the regional centers and project developers who pay them to find EB-5 investors—and may not even completely understand the projects he or she is advertising, so it is important to carefully perform "due diligence" on migration agents before you hire one.

The most important things you should look for in a migration agent include the agent's track record in EB-5 and whether the agent is being paid by multiple players in the EB-5 industry, including you, the regional center, and/or the project developer. While migration agents will charge you a fee for finding EB-5 projects, they may also get commission from the regional center and/ or developer for raising EB-5 capital, so you want to make sure that they are directing you to a project that is right for you, not just a project that will make them more money. When hiring a migration agent, you should ask to have this information fully disclosed—if a migration agent refuses to disclose this information, you should not hire this person. Chapter 3 will provide you with a detailed list of what to look for when you are hiring the professionals that will help you with your EB-5 process.

There are ways of finding EB-5 projects without hiring a migration agent, which may save you money. However, many investors choose to hire a migration agent to make the process more manageable and to be sure that they have a knowledgeable ally to walk them through all the steps in the migration process. It is possible to find a project on your own, but a migration agent can make this step much easier.

IMMIGRATION ATTORNEY

If you use a migration agent, that agent (or the regional center itself) will usually refer you to an experienced EB-5 immigration attorney. However, you should only hire an immigration attorney who is licensed to practice in the United States. Because of this, your migration agent may be your main point of contact with your immigration attorney until you move to the United States. It is important that the attorney you hire has a successful track record in EB-5 cases to increase your likelihood of getting a green card; working with an inexperienced EB-5 immigration attorney is not recommended. In many cases, immigration attorneys work with translators or have foreign language speakers in their offices, so do not worry about being unable to communicate with an English-speaking immigration attorney. They know that many of their clients do not speak English, and most have prepared for this by having individuals in their offices to translate your native language into English.

Your immigration attorney will help you prepare all the forms necessary to document your investment and job creation and apply for your green card. Apart from helping you prepare your visa application, your immigration attorney may sometimes introduce you to EB-5 projects, especially if he or she works closely with regional centers. They may not be able to tell you which project is best for you in the financial sense, but they may be able to make introductions for you. Unless your immigration attorney has the proper licensing to advise and recommend your financial decisions (very few do), you may want to instead meet with an investment adviser (explained shortly) to help guide you in these types of decisions.

Tip

Conflict of Interest: If you work with a project or regional center before you hire an immigration attorney, they may recommend an immigration attorney to you. The goal is to have an unbiased attorney who looks after your best interests. Before you hire any attorney associated with a particular regional center or project, ask the attorney whether he or she represents the project or regional center in any way. It is important to know whether there are any potential conflicts of interest if the attorney is representing both you and the regional center or project. If the immigration attorney properly discloses his or her relationship with regional centers and their EB-5 projects, you do not necessarily need to view this relationship negatively.

When hiring an immigration attorney, always strive to fully understand his or her relationship with a regional center and receive a complete disclosure of any fees paid to the immigration attorney by the regional center or developer before hiring him or her. Your immigration attorney will play a huge role throughout your entire EB-5 experience, which can take over five years to complete, so hiring the appropriate immigration attorney is incredibly important to your success as an EB-5 investor. Consider hiring an attorney whose first focus is on helping you immigrate.

REGImONAL CENTER

You have already read a little bit about regional centers and know that a regional center is a government approved entity involved with the promotion of economic growth and job creation. Regional centers are usually involved with projects that have multiple investors. Unless the investment is a direct investment—which is a small fraction of EB-5 deals—project developers affiliate with a regional center to have the benefit of counting indirect and induced jobs. So it is highly likely that you will be working with a regional center. Essentially, you will be investing under a regional center, not in a regional center.

Each regional center is approved for a specific region of the United States. Bear in mind, however, that USCIS approval of a regional center does not in any way endorse the activities of the regional center, guarantee that the regional center complies with US securities laws, or eliminate immigration risk for you as an investor. Currently, there are more than 450 USCIS-designated regional centers, and this number continues to grow. On the USCIS website, there is a comprehensive list of USCIS-designated regional centers for you to explore. As an EB-5 investor, there are a variety of ways to get in contact with regional centers, so don't feel tied down to one method for getting in touch with regional centers. To find regional center investment opportunities, you can call or visit the websites of different regional centers, you can speak with your migration agent for specific recommendations (if you hire a migration agent), or you can speak with your immigration attorney about regional centers with which he or she is familiar.

Additionally, regional centers are responsible for understanding the immigration component of your investment and complying with USCIS regulations, which can help ensure that your investment actually qualifies you for a green card through EB-5. In fact, the regional center will interact with a team of industry professionals in EB-5, including economists, immigration attorneys, business plan writers, and migration agents, to verify that the project follows the guidelines of the EB-5 program.

Tip

At Risk: In the EB-5 program, all investments are required to be "at risk," which means that there must be some chance you can lose your entire investment, so any regional centers or projects that make promises or guarantees should be approached with caution.

PROJECT DEVELOPER

With EB-5, there is always a project developer (sometimes called a project sponsor). The project developer is the person (or company) in charge of the project you will be investing in, and it is the one that uses your money to build its business and create (or in very limited circumstances, preserve) jobs.

If the regional center is developing its own project, the regional center and developer, in simple terms, are the same owner. This is often seen in the EB-5 world. In other cases, a third-party developer may approach a regional center to ask for help raising EB-5 money. In this arrangement the regional center and project developer are unaffiliated entities.

When promoting EB-5 projects, project developers themselves will often attend conferences or seminars in your home country, with or without their regional center partners, where you can ask them in-depth, specific questions about their EB-5 projects. After all, no one knows the projects better than the developers. Note that your success depends on the project's success because your money is invested in the project. Also, a project that is a financial failure may not create the jobs you need for your green card. Factors to look at, which will be discussed later, are track record and credibility of the developer. You are entrusting your investment and immigration success to them. Remember that developers' primary strength is in developing projects—not EB-5 matters—so their knowledge of the immigration process can be sparse. You may need to address questions about the EB-5 program to your migration agent or immigration attorney or directly to the regional center.

INVESTMENT ADVISER

You may or may not come into contact with an investment adviser (or broker-dealer). This is a person who will help guide your investment decisions from a financial risk perspective. Some investors hire these individuals to review different regional centers and their respective projects before choosing a specific project in which to invest. In fact, some investment advisers will give potential investors a "menu" of EB-5 projects to choose from.

An investment adviser will answer the question, "What is the probability that I will receive the returns projected in the offering documents and receive my money back at the end of the EB-5 process?" This is an important question to ask. Also the adviser should look at the job-creation requirement of your investment. As noted above, an unsuccessful project may not create all the jobs you need, so financial strength, although not your top priority, still plays a vital role in evaluating EB-5 projects. Projects that have been reviewed and deemed suitable by competent and independent investment advisers may offer a lower level of investment and, therefore, immigration risk—however, this suitability determination does not replace your own due diligence review of a project. Investment advisers generally must be registered with the US Securities and Exchange Commission (SEC) or the states in which they operate and they should be well-versed in the laws affecting EB-5 investments.

You can hire an investment adviser (or broker-dealer) independently to consult on an EB-5 project's viability. The investment adviser should first determine your specific investment interests and help you determine which EB-5 projects are financially sound. These individuals typically have a limited foreign presence, which means you may need to hire one that operates within the United States. In the current EB-5 market, hiring investment advisers is becoming more popular.

OTHER KEY PLAYERS

There is another group of key players who are important to the EB-5 process who you will likely not come into contact with if you are investing under an EB-5 regional center—economists, business plan writers, and securities attorneys. It is nonetheless important that you understand a bit about their roles in the EB-5 process so that you can be empowered to ask the right questions of your EB-5 team. The regional center (or project developer) hires these individuals for assistance before beginning to accept EB-5 capital. These are the team members who will work together behind the scenes to increase the likelihood that your project will be financially successful. These other players are described in *Table B*.

Table B

Visas with Immigrant Status	
Securities Attorney	A securities attorney will work for the project you are investing in and advises the project on the process of selling you ownership interests in the EB-5 project entity in conformity with US securities laws and other laws affecting business entities in the US. You will probably have to sign documents drafted by securities attorneys, so you should know the basics of who they are and what they do.
Business Plan Writer	A business plan writer is responsible for writing a business plan for the project. Business plan writers try to ensure that the business plan complies with USCIS regulations and keep EB-5 visa requirements in mind. A solid business plan can be the difference between approval and denial of your green card.
Economist	You will probably not meet the economist, but you will hear about this person during the EB-5 process. Regional centers (or project sponsors) hire economists to estimate job creation for their EB-5 projects, and this directly affects whether you receive your green card. The economist forecasts job creation in an economic impact study, and this study tells USCIS if it is possible and likely that your investment will create at least 10 jobs for US workers. Similarly, the economist can analyze if a project is located in a targeted employment area (TEA). Projects located in TEAs require a $500,000 investment as opposed to $1 million, which can save you money if you decide to invest in one of these projects.

CONCLUSION

As you can see, you may come into contact with a variety of individuals, all of whom contribute to the EB-5 process in some way. When you come into contact with any of these key players, it will be your job to make sure all of the proper information is disclosed so that you can set yourself up for immigration and investment success in the EB-5 program. Now that you have met all the key players, it is time to move on and determine whether the EB-5 program is right for you.

The EB-5 Handbook

CHAPTER 2: WHERE DO I BEGIN?

By Al Rattan and Kevin Wright

If becoming a permanent resident through the EB-5 visa program sounds like the right immigration option for you, the first step is to understand the requirements to determine whether you are eligible for the program. After determining your eligibility, you will then need to find projects to consider investing in. In order to avoid hassle, you should consider your eligibility before attempting to file any paperwork with USCIS. An immigration attorney can help you navigate this process, but this chapter discusses some basic information on these issues before going down the EB-5 road yourself.

UNDERSTANDING THE REQUIREMENTS

There are four major requirements you must meet to receive your green card in the EB-5 program:

1. Make an "at risk" investment of at least $500,000 (or $1 million, depending on whether the investment is in a TEA).

2. Prove that your investment funds were obtained lawfully;

3. Create (or in very limited circumstances, preserve) 10 jobs for US workers over a two-year period; and

4. Be in some form of management position in the business.

When you make an "at risk" investment, this means that there is some chance that you will lose your entire investment. While this is not what most investors experience in the EB-5 program, it is a risk that you must be aware of and agree to assume.

In terms of job creation, you are not personally responsible for finding and hiring these 10 workers, but your investment capital should create a need for these 10 jobs (e.g., creating jobs for the construction workers who build a hotel project you invest in or for those who work in the hotel after it is built). You and your family members immigrating with you do not count towards this number. If using the regional center option, you will be able to count indirect and induced jobs towards your required 10 jobs. These indirect or induced jobs are created as an indirect result of the investment.

Your immigration attorney will help you document how your investment was obtained lawfully, which usually includes providing USCIS with bank statements and other credible sources that document your finances. The government wants to make sure that your investment was not earned illegally by selling drugs, engaging in terrorist activities, or other illegal means. For more information about documenting your funds, read *Chapter 4.*

Whether you invest directly or under a regional center, you must be in some sort of active management or policy-making position in the business. With direct investments (that are not pooled or syndicated), you will normally be in a more direct management role (this would include day-to-day management of the business), which is why many investors prefer investing under regional centers where the management requirement is more flexible. With regional center investments, your managerial responsibilities are typically quite low (your role will be more passive, with your responsibilities focusing more on policy-making decisions that do not require you to be in charge of operating the business). You will learn more about managerial responsibilities in this chapter.

Your immigration attorney will help you document how you have met these requirements in order to show this to USCIS as evidence.

EB-5 ELIGIBILITY

The EB-5 program has some of the same basic eligibility requirements as other visa programs. This includes a background check to ensure applicants have not committed certain crimes, do not have a history of financial fraud, and have not previously violated immigration laws. However, one huge advantage of the EB-5 program is its lack of requirements that may otherwise restrict your ability to immigrate, as compared to other visas. Here are some of the notable differences:

- There is no need for family members in the United States to sponsor you.
- There is no need for an employer in the United States to sponsor you.
- There is no minimum required proficiency in the English language.
- There is no required skill set, training, or education.

This means that the EB-5 program can be a good option for investors who do not meet the more specific requirements of other immigration pathways. However, EB-5 is just as stringent with background checks as other visa pathways, and it is equally vulnerable to security concerns or fraud. EB-5 also has its own specific requirements that must be considered, the most important of which is your financial eligibility.

Financial Eligibility

The most obvious hurdle is the need for capital: $500,000 or $1 million to invest into an EB-5 project. It's not as simple as stuffing $1 million into an envelope and mailing it to the United States; this money has its own requirements. The USCIS needs to be sure this money came from a lawful source.

Where Can My Capital Come From? As an EB-5 investor, your capital must be immediately available and legally-sourced. This means that the entirety of your investment capital must be committed to a project (most often in an escrow account) before applying for your two-year conditional green card, and those funds must also have been earned through lawful means. These funds can come from a variety of sources, including, but not limited to:

- salary earned through lawful employment
- gifts of money from family members, friends, employers, etc.
- retirement accounts and pensions
- profits made selling a house, real estate, or other assets
- a loan (as long as the loan has collateral and a responsibility on the investor to pay back)

It is not enough for you to know that your funds were acquired legally—your immigration attorney must be able to clearly document the source of your funds for USCIS to review. In order to prove that no illegal activity was used to gain these funds, USCIS requires a large amount of information, typically including, but not limited to:

- foreign business registration records
- personal and business tax returns or other tax returns of any kind filed anywhere in the world within the last five years
- documents identifying any other sources of money
- certified copies of all pending civil or criminal cases involving money judgments against you within the past 15 years
- similar documents showing sources of funds for money received through gifts

Basically, these requirements help ensure that foreign investors are not attempting to exploit the EB-5 program. These requirements also ensure that only lawful, legally operating investors are able to immigrate. Collecting these documents is an involved process and one that most often requires the assistance of an immigration attorney experienced with EB-5. Otherwise, USCIS might request more evidence to document your source of funds, or it may deny your application altogether.

Tip

Gifting Capital: It is perfectly legal to gift the required capital to one of your children for him or her to participate in EB-5. He or she would still, however, have to prove that the money you gifted was legally sourced. This is a strategy that many foreign nationals use to help start their children on the path to US residency. Under current US law, this strategy would also allow you to join your adult child in the United States under a family-based visa if your child eventually applied for US citizenship, which would be a minimum of five years after your child received a green card, then sponsored you for a green card as an "immediate relative." Gifts can also be made by unrelated parties to the investor.

How Much Capital Do I Need? Most projects will only require an investment (not counting administrative fees) of $500,000 because most projects are located in TEAs. Those who are offering EB-5 projects know that you will likely not be interested in investing $1 million for their project when you can invest $500,000 in someone else's project and likely receive the same outcome: a green card. On the other hand, if you are actively looking to start and run your own business, it may make less of a difference to you whether you invest $500,000 or $1 million if you own the entire business.

Whether investing $500,000 or $1 million, there is no guarantee that any of this money will be returned to you. You might be able to obtain a green card without ever getting your money back or get your money back without a green card. The two things to consider are investment success and immigration success.

When Do I Have to Make My Investment? Although USCIS regulations seem to say otherwise, the full amount of your investment must typically be committed to the project, usually in an escrow account before you can file your application. Most projects use an escrow account, but it is not required for EB-5. Remember, an escrow account is a third-party bank account that will hold onto your money until certain terms of the escrow agreement you sign with the regional center are met. Your immigration attorney or investment adviser can discuss with you different strategies of investing your funds. While you may be able to find a project that will not actually use your funds until your visa application (I-526) is approved, it is more likely that some of the funds will be released to the project before all I-526 approvals have been obtained, as the time for I-526 approvals can be as long as 18 months. (You have to review the offering documents of the specific project to determine whether your funds will be held in escrow, and if so, when they will be released. Your immigration attorney or investment adviser can help you review those documents.) This requirement (committing your investment before I-526 approval) is in place to prove that you are financially and personally invested in this project.

Will I Get My Money Back? The laws governing the EB-5 program state that your investment must be "at risk," meaning that, as in all true investments, there may be some chance that you will lose some or all of your investment. But don't let this requirement steer you away from EB-5; if you do your homework and consult the proper professionals throughout the EB-5 process, you should have a high probability of receiving your green card. But receiving your green card does not mean that you will have all of your money returned to you. EB-5 requires your investment to be at risk, so there is no guarantee you will see the full amount of your investment returned. Presently, only a handful of regional centers have been in the field long enough to have a successful track record for returning investors' funds, but this number is rapidly growing. Because EB-5 is a relatively new visa option, and the timeline for completing EB-5 projects and receiving green cards can take about five years, many EB-5 projects are currently in the process of returning funds to investors.

What Other Costs Can I Expect to Pay? Besides the minimum $500,000 investment, there are other costs you can expect to pay as you participate in the EB-5 program. Some of these costs are absolutely necessary to the immigration process, such as the fees you will have to pay for the processing of your forms with USCIS (the table below includes the standard costs from USCIS). Since the industry does not have standard fees for attorneys and regional centers, we have opted not to create a chart. Most deals depend on many factors outside the scope of this book, so it is best to shop and compare attorneys and regional centers. However, as a basic range, currently regional centers charge an administrative fee of approximately $50,000 and immigration attorneys charge in the range of $25,000. Services vary depending on which attorney or regional center you are using, so these numbers are merely estimates.

Filing Costs with USCIS	
I-526	$1,500
I-485	$985 (plus an $85 biometrics fee)
I-829	$3,750 (plus an $85 biometrics fee)

What is the Process for Me and My Family to Get Green Cards? If your I-526 is approved, you can then file for your two-year "conditional" green card. You do this one of two ways, depending on whether you will be applying from outside of the United States (which is most common in EB-5) or will be applying from within the United States (i.e., if you are already in the United States in some other nonimmigrant status, such as with a student visa or work visa). The first process is called "consular processing," and the other option is called "adjustment of status."

If you are outside the United States and will be consular processing, USCIS will notify the National Visa Center in the United States that your I-526 petition was approved and that you will be applying for your two-conditional green card in your home country. (If you have long-term status in another country, you might consular process in that country instead, but most of the time, you will consular process in your own country.) You then will pay filing fees and complete an online form called a DS-260. After that, you will prepare for your visa interview at the consulate. If that goes well, then you will be issued an immigrant visa to travel to the United States to begin your two-year conditional green card period.

On the other hand, if you are in the United States in a nonimmigrant visa status, such as student or work status, when your I-526 petition is approved, then you will typically complete the green card processing in the United States. You do this by filing a Form I-485 (Application to Register Permanent Residence or Adjust Status) with the appropriate USCIS office, along with the filing fees and supporting documentation. Upon I-485 approval, you will be issued your two-year conditional green card.

When Will I Get my *Permanent* Green Card? Irrespective of whether you obtained your two-year conditional green card through consular processing or adjustment of status, you eventually have to file to convert that conditional green card into a permanent one. To make this conversion, you will have to submit a Form I-829 (Petition by Entrepreneur to Remove Conditions), which has a filing fee of $3,750. The I-829 petition also requires a biometrics fee of $85 for the investor and each family member (14 years of age or older) included on the application. The biometrics process involves taking your fingerprints and taking your photograph.

If you have determined that you are eligible for the EB-5 program, the next step is to determine what type of investment you will make.

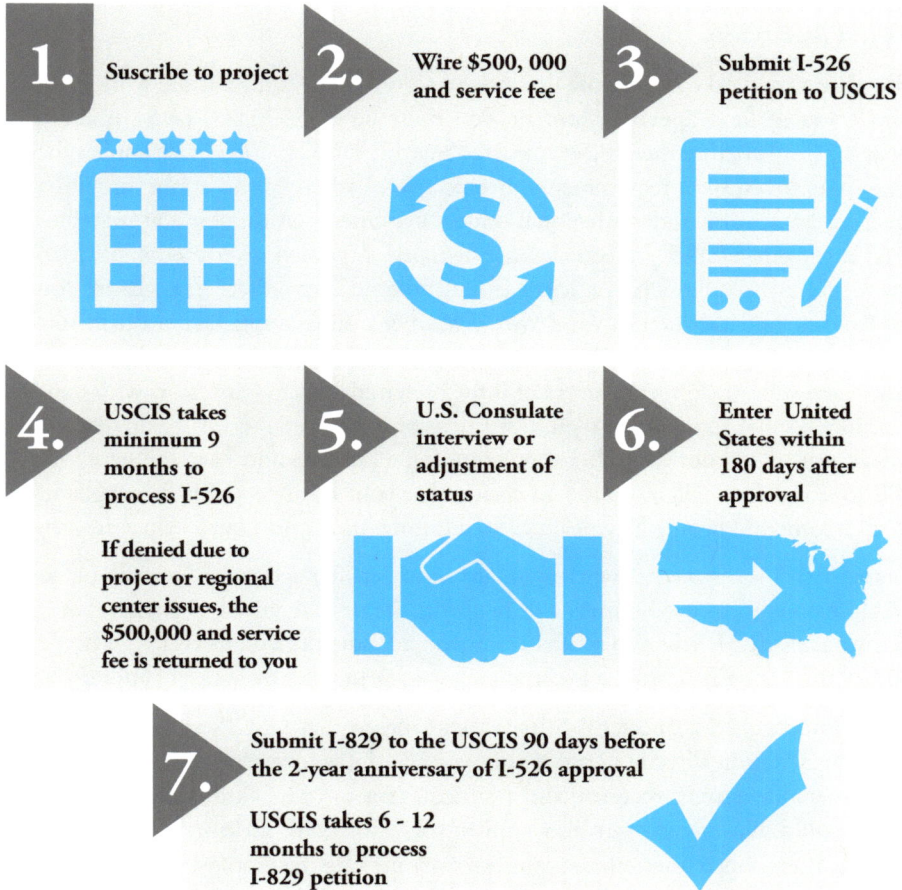

1. Suscribe to project
2. Wire $500, 000 and service fee
3. Submit I-526 petition to USCIS
4. USCIS takes minimum 9 months to process I-526

If denied due to project or regional center issues, the $500,000 and service fee is returned to you
5. U.S. Consulate interview or adjustment of status
6. Enter United States within 180 days after approval
7. Submit I-829 to the USCIS 90 days before the 2-year anniversary of I-526 approval

USCIS takes 6 - 12 months to process I-829 petition

DECIDING HOW TO INVEST: DIRECT OR INDIRECT

There are two main EB-5 investment options for you to consider: direct investment and indirect investment (i.e., investing under a regional center). The majority of investors choose to make indirect investments, and most regional-center projects qualify for the lesser $500,000 amount. The decision typically determines how much control (and therefore responsibility) over the project you want to have. While both kinds of investment require you to be a member of management or be in a policy-making position, the level of this involvement will vary. Your investment choice also affects how USCIS will count the jobs necessary for the EB-5 requirement. Both have their advantages and disadvantages, and you should consider your own goals and skill sets when making this choice.

Direct Investment

The direct method can be more expensive and typically requires more work from you. If you make a direct investment, you must invest $500,000 or $1 million, depending on whether the project is located in a TEA (i.e., the TEA rule applies the same to all investment requirements, irrespective of whether you apply through a direct investment or under a regional center investment). Although you may find some larger direct EB-5 projects that are operated as pooled investments in which you would not play much of a management role, in most direct EB-5 cases, you will have to find or develop your own investment project and take a direct role managing and overseeing it. Fewer than 15 percent of EB-5 investors choose this route. Generally, the direct investment is the preferred choice of investors who want to maintain some control over their investment on a day-to-day basis. To do this will require you to be knowledgeable about running a business and have the necessary skills to do so. You will also need to ensure that your business is EB-5 compliant, which is something you will typically hire an immigration attorney to help you with.

Direct EB-5 investments (where you are active in management) require you to live close enough to the business and to spend the time required to ensure that it operates as planned. This also means that it will be more difficult to visit your home country until the EB-5 process is complete, which can takes five years or more.

More importantly, a direct EB-5 investment means that USCIS will only count those jobs that you directly create within your business towards your job creation requirement (assuming that you did not acquire a so-called "troubled business," which would allow you—but also require you—to "save" at least 10 jobs). For example, if you open a restaurant, you can only include the employees within that restaurant, such as the servers, the cooks, and the hosts. Because the vast majority of EB-5 investors choose the regional center approach instead of the direct approach, the major focus of this book will be the regional center approach.

Tip

Direct Jobs: In the EB-5 visa program, you cannot include yourself or any of your family members in the job count number.

Indirect Investment (Regional Center Investment)

Managerial Responsibilities. If you don't feel you have the time or expertise to start and operate a new business in the United States on your own, especially with a business and tax climate that might be substantially different from that of your home country, then the regional center indirect investment approach is likely a better fit for you. If you choose to make an indirect investment, you will still have to be in some kind of policy-making position of the new commercial enterprise as a "limited partner" or as a "member." Your responsibilities will be minimal but may include voting at owner meetings, helping advise on policy decisions, or engaging in other rather passive duties that do not require you to be in charge of the day-to-day operations of the business. The paperwork you sign with the regional center's new commercial enterprise will tell you what your managerial responsibilities will be.

If you select a good regional center and EB-5 project to invest in, you should find yourself guided along the EB-5 path by a team of professionals, and you won't worry much about attending to the day-to-day operations of the project directly. *Chapter 3* will give you the tools you need to evaluate regional centers and their available EB-5 projects.

With an indirect investment, you have little control over the project (and therefore less responsibility). This may seem like bad news. The good news is that without heavy burdens for you to attend to at the project entity, you will have much more time to conduct your own affairs.

Indirect and Induced Job Creation. Perhaps most importantly of all, as previously mentioned, a regional center-based EB-5 investment allows you to count not only "direct" job creation, but also "indirect" and "induced" job creation. When you make an indirect investment, regional center projects can use established economic models to estimate how many jobs will be created through the economic boost from the project's success.

Indirect jobs created by the project as it purchases supplies. Induced jobs created when employees of the project spend their money.

"Indirect" jobs are created when local businesses need to hire more workers to provide your EB-5 project with the supplies and labor it needs to be completed. For example, if the project needs wood from a lumber company, and that company has to hire a truck driver to deliver the wood to the project site, then the job of the newly hired truck driver is an indirect job.

Induced jobs are created when all of the workers considered "direct" or "indirect" employment go into the local economy to buy goods and services from other providers (e.g., food, movies, dry cleaning, or autos). Although job creation is critical for your EB-5 case, it is also somewhat complicated. The economist hired by the regional center will conduct the necessary calculations to determine the number of jobs that will be created by your investment and will prepare a detailed economic report to explain the job creation calculations to USCIS.

Because you can count direct, indirect, and induced jobs within a regional center-based investment, the regional center's project will be deemed to create more jobs and can therefore support more EB-5 investors for the same amount of capital invested.

FINDING AN EB-5 PROJECT

If you decide that a regional center-based investment is the right way for you to proceed, then the next step is to actually find a project to invest in. There are several ways that you can do this, but each option will fit into one of two categories: doing it yourself or finding someone to help you.

Doing It Yourself

If you have the time to commit to finding an EB-5 project independently, there are options available to you. Whether you are ready to invest or just want to find more information about specific projects before committing to EB-5, finding projects through the Internet and web directories can be a good option for you. This can also be a good way to get a feel for EB-5 projects in general. Additionally, this process will help develop your understanding of how the program works, which will further help in trying to analyze your options and select an appropriate process. The goal of *The EB-5 Handbook* is to help you with this effort.

Regional Centers. You can call or visit the websites of individual regional centers to find out more about the types of projects they specialize in. Normally, you can also come to the United States to visit the site of an EB-5 project. If this is something you would like to do, consult the regional center or project developer to make sure you are not violating any immigration or securities regulations. Also speak with your immigration attorney about temporarily traveling to the United States and whether you need to complete any extra steps before you visit. If you find a regional center that you may be interested in investing with, you should always double check that it is approved by USCIS by checking the USCIS website or asking to see the regional center's designation letter from USCIS. USCIS provides a complete list of approved regional centers, which is updated periodically. However, USCIS approval of an EB-5 regional center does not mean that USCIS endorses that regional center. It only means that the regional center can legally operate as an EB-5 regional center, which is the first due diligence question you should ask in the process (see Chapter 3 for a more detailed discussion of the due diligence process).

Finding Projects with Professional Assistance

If you would rather have professionals experienced in EB-5 help you—or if you have not been able to find enough information in your own research—you can hire and consult with different kinds of EB-5 professionals to find projects. The most notable professionals include migration agents, immigration attorneys, finders, and US-based investment advisers who perform "due diligence" services.

Migration Agents. Using a migration agent is the most popular way for investors to find EB-5 projects, especially Chinese investors. As mentioned in Chapter 1, a migration agent is someone who is licensed outside of the United States to offer citizens of foreign countries immigration options. It is typical to talk to a migration agent before talking to an immigration attorney, although it isn't necessary. While a migration agent can be very helpful in finding a good regional center and project, you should carefully research the agent (or agency) before hiring anyone.

Remember that you are not the only one who pays migration agents for their services—EB-5 regional centers and project developers also pay them to find investors for their projects. This means there may be a conflict of interest. Sometimes, migration agents will recommend the EB-5 project of a developer who pays them the most money, regardless of whether the project is likely to succeed. You should ask your potential migration agent what he or she typically charges a regional center and what kind of due diligence, or investigation, has been done on the EB-5 project. Make sure there are legitimate reasons why the migration agent is promoting a particular project.

One valuable benefit to migration agents is that they are locally available to you and can help you select and invest in an EB-5 project. An experienced migration agent has worked with a lot of EB-5 investors before and can help you navigate many of the steps of the immigration process. Moreover, many of these migration agents may also give you immigration options for other countries, which may help you decide whether the EB-5 program is the best fit for you.

Immigration Attorneys. Licensed to practice law in the United States, an immigration attorney is another professional who can assist you in finding EB-5 projects. Bear in mind that a license to practice law is not a license to make investment recommendations on EB-5 projects. Moreover, immigration attorneys are typically not trained in financial investments and normally should not advise your financial decisions. They can, however, give you a list of regional centers (and their contact information) and discuss their own personal experiences with those regional centers. They can also give you advice on due diligence for the projects, but they should not recommend a particular project to you from a financial perspective.

Watch out for any potential conflicts of interest with your immigration attorney. Make sure you fully understand your immigration attorney's relationship with any regional centers or projects, and make sure you know what kinds of fees he or she is receiving from the regional centers or projects before you hire the attorney. Some immigration attorneys have helped set up EB-5 regional centers and EB-5 projects, which means that they may refer you to projects that they want to be financially successful rather than ones that will fulfill your immigration requirements. However, if the immigration attorney discloses his or her relationship with these projects or regional centers, then it may not necessarily be a bad thing. It just requires a little more due diligence on your part. There may also be a conflict of interest if the immigration attorney accepts a fee from a regional center or project in exchange for referring you. You want to make sure that your immigration attorney is committed to your interests above the interests of the regional center or project developer.

Another potential conflict of interest can happen if the immigration attorney actually owns the regional center in which you are considering investing. In this case, it is highly unlikely the attorney will be able to properly represent your interests and the regional center's interests at the same time. Many recognized experts in immigration law and rules of professional responsibility strongly recommend against such lawyers representing investors in their own projects, so you should probably not hire such lawyers either. (Please note that immigration lawyers owning regional centers is not by itself a concern; the concern is that they own the one that you are actually investing in. That is likely a serious conflict of interest.)

Finders. Finders are anyone (professional or nonprofessional) who happens to refer you to a regional center or project. Sometimes in limited circumstances, regional centers may pay such finders a fee for referring you. Other times, they won't because paying such a finder's fee to such a person may violate US securities laws.

US-Licensed Investment Professionals. Although not very common, there are some US-licensed investment professionals who provide "due diligence" reviews on many of the most recent EB-5 projects. Some may provide due diligence on a non-commission basis, but it is also important to determine whether the investment professional is also being paid by the regional center or project for making the referral to that project.

CONCLUSION

The EB-5 program offers benefits to potential immigrants that other programs may not, but it also has different requirements. If you decide that the EB-5 visa program sounds like the best way for you to immigrate to the United States, the first thing you must do is understand the requirements of the program and make sure you are financially eligible.

Then, you should decide whether you want to invest your capital towards creating your own business on an active basis or simply invest indirectly under a regional center. While the indirect method is the most popular, the direct method also has its own advantages.

If you decide to invest via the regional center-based approach, your next step is to find a regional center and project. You can do a lot of research on your own and contact regional centers directly, or you can hire someone to help you with this process and advise you on what to look for.

When all this is done, you should have a variety of potential regional centers and projects to choose from. The following chapter discusses the next step—choosing and evaluating the project that you will invest in.

CHAPTER 3: IS THIS A GOOD PROJECT?
By Al Rattan and Kyle Walker

Now that you may have some projects or regional centers in mind, it is time to choose which one is right for you. The next steps will require you to do careful research and work with experienced professionals to make sure that you are investing in a safe project that will meet the requirements of EB-5. Choosing a good project will give you the greatest chance of receiving your green card and getting the full amount of your investment back after the end of the immigration process. As with any investment or business venture, you should do your own due diligence review of a project and the players involved before investing. By their very nature, there are no guarantees with EB-5 investments (remember, USCIS requires EB-5 investments to be "at-risk"), so looking at all of the information available to you will reduce the risk of making a poor investment decision.

Due diligence is the process of investigating a project (and the people associated with the project) for strengths and risk factors as they relate to your investment and your immigration prospects. It is a process of gathering the facts you need to decide whether a project is likely to fulfill your immigration and financial goals. You want to do it right the first time—this will take some work. The good thing is that you don't have to do it alone. Before you even come into the EB-5 picture, most—if not all—EB-5 projects have been reviewed by many people, so it is important to understand how (and if) projects have been reviewed before you found them. It is also important to remember that there are many good EB-5 projects sponsored by reputable developers and regional centers, so do not be too concerned about finding the *absolutely best one*. It is more important to find the project that is *best for you.*

DUE DILIGENCE BY THE REGIONAL CENTER

As discussed earlier, regional centers offer a variety of projects for you to invest in. Regional center owners will either work with developers of outside projects who are looking for funding, or they will develop their own projects for investors. When working with outside project developers, a reputable regional center will conduct a due diligence review of the developer's project before it begins offering it to investors. Regional center due diligence usually looks at the project's budget and projections, the background of the project's principals (the people who are in charge of the project and important to it), an appraisal, the land deed, and corporate documents.

Regional centers know that your primary reason for investing is immigration, so the ability of a project to create at least 10 jobs per investor (to fulfill your immigration requirement) is one of the most important things for the regional center to consider when doing a due diligence review of a project. To determine job creation, regional centers will hire an independent economist to create an economic impact report. The economist's report supports the regional center's projected number of US jobs for EB-5 visa requirements. Some regional centers will even internally analyze the job creation prospects, the market, and the likelihood of the project's success. Regional center due diligence may include 100 or more documents. The business plan summarizes how the project will use your money and how it will create the jobs you need to satisfy your EB-5 requirements.

While it is necessary for the regional center to review all of the documents, some documents are confidential, so many developers are cautious to share such information with interested investors. Regional centers have to protect their own interests and those of other investors. Once you commit to an EB-5 project, you may have access to more confidential information that is only shared with investment partners. Remember that regional centers want their projects to succeed as well, and it makes them look good if you are able to successfully get your investment back and immigrate to the United States, so their due diligence is worth looking at.

YOUR OWN DUE DILIGENCE

A regional center's due diligence review does not replace the need for your own evaluation of an EB-5 project or the people involved in the process. You will need to evaluate the regional center, its projects, and the people you will work with. Before you can trust the due diligence review offered by a regional center, it is important that you make sure the regional center itself is reputable. You should always conduct a due diligence review yourself (with the assistance of your trusted advisers) to increase your chances of immigration and investment success. This point cannot be emphasized enough: take the time to do a due diligence review of each individual you work with, as one slip up can jeopardize your prospects of receiving a green card. When considering any EB-5 project, evaluate the key players involved in the project (see Chapter 1 for a discussion of the most important players in EB-5 for you to know as an investor). Getting to know these individuals will help you decide whether the project they represent will meet your EB-5 requirements. When you are deciding who to work with, keep in mind that you will likely be working with them throughout the EB-5 process, portions of which take years. Have patience in the beginning to conduct as much due diligence as you reasonably can so that you make the best possible decisions.

Developers, Regional Centers, and Consultants

Often, a project is independent from the regional center; they are not necessarily related entities. Relationships between regional centers and project developers can take on a variety of forms. In some cases, for example, the regional center may sponsor a project through a shared services agreement in which the developers are responsible for project documentation, raising capital (accepting investments), USCIS compliance, and SEC compliance. In other cases, project developers may go to a regional center to request a loan for their business and the regional center will prepare all necessary documentation, raise capital, comply with USCIS and SEC regulations, and act as lender to the project. In other cases, regional centers will develop their own projects for investors. In any case, learning who you will be working with is important before committing to an EB-5 project.

Get to Know the Project Developers. No one will know the project better than the developers, but as noted in Chapter 1, project developers are normally not well-versed in EB-5 matters. Their knowledge of the project typically does not include important immigration questions that you need answered. However, they should have a good understanding of the financial aspects of their project and can answer your questions about financial return and an exit strategy. When getting to know project developers, you should find out their track record with development projects in general; that is, if their past projects were completed on time, if they were financially successful, and the timeframes to exit. These questions will help you predict if the project developer will construct and develop your EB-5 project according to the timeline outlined in the business plan—projects that are not developed according to the business plan may result in the denial of removed conditions at the I-829 stage (when you request your permanent green card) because USCIS imposes time requirements for job creation. Similarly, you should know how much equity the developer has invested in the project. If the developer has not invested its own equity, it will have less incentive to ensure that the project is successful. Lack of developer capital may also be a sign that the developer does not believe in the financial success of the project and/or that the developer may not be willing or able to deploy additional capital to the project, if needed. Generally speaking, a developer who invests at least 20 percent of its own capital should be viewed positively, although 30 percent is even more preferable. Even if the developer has a healthy 20 to 30 percent equity stake in the project, when

EB-5 capital represents all of the additional capital in the capital stack (i.e., the project is funded 70 percent or more with EB-5 capital), it may be a risk factor. Percentages of EB-5 capital of 70 or more may indicate that other third party funding sources, such as bank senior lenders or equity partners, declined to fund the project. The lack of other lending or equity sources may also be a problem in the future if the project needs more capital due to unforeseen circumstances, such as construction delay or a severe recession that delays revenue stabilization. Finally, you should be cautious of projects that require all EB-5 capital to be released to the project before I-526 adjudication, without providing a back-up source of funds to reimburse investors whose I-526s are denied.

Get to Know the Regional Center Operators. Regional center operators should be well-versed in EB-5 and USCIS immigration requirements, but they tend to be less knowledgeable about the particulars of specific EB-5 projects (unless they are also developing the project). Regional center operators should do thorough due diligence of EB-5 projects through their service provider team, which includes immigration attorneys, business plan writers, economists, and other individuals knowledgeable in EB-5 requirements. Regional centers should be willing to share the names of their professionals, and you should perform due diligence on these professionals. You should always be aware that a regional center's retention of a reputable professional does not imply an endorsement of the project by that professional. Professionals work for the project and not for the investors, and their engagements frequently contain limitations on their scope of work. The one exception to this warning is registered broker-dealers. The regulatory body for broker-dealers (FINRA) requires them to perform due diligence on projects they represent, so due diligence cannot be carved out of their scope of services. This is one of the main reasons the involvement of a broker-dealer is beneficial to investors.

When getting to know regional center operators, you should look at their track record in EB-5: how many I-526 approvals can they show you? How many I-829 approvals can they show you? Have they had any denials of these forms with past projects? However, not every regional center will be able to share this information with you, and you do not necessarily need to view this negatively. Because EB-5 regional centers are relatively new to the EB-5 visa program and many regional centers are currently getting USCIS designation, they may not have a successful track record to share with you—when this is the case, you should take the regional center operators' backgrounds into consideration and whether they have experienced success in their respective fields. This should be a good indication of how they will operate in the EB-5 world.

Get to Know the EB-5 Consultants. Project developers will sometimes hire EB-5 marketing consultants to market the project. Consultants should have a good understanding of both sides of the equation (yours and the regional center's/ developer's), but are often not experts in project development or in running a regional center. Because consultants' reputations hinge on the success of the projects they represent, they tend to do quite a bit of their own due diligence themselves and choose projects cautiously, which often makes them good sources of information, and you should always ask for full disclosure of their compensation and take that into account with respect to their recommendations. Marketing consultants are usually compensated based on their success in raising funds. In other words, if you invest, they will earn commissions and fees based on your investment. Those commissions may be 15 percent of your investment or more. These consultants therefore have a significant conflict of interest, and the extent of that conflict (that is, the full fees they earn) may not be clearly disclosed (or indeed disclosed at all) in the offering documents. You should evaluate EB-5 consultants based on their experience and the success of past projects they have worked with.

Due diligence does not end with just getting to know the experience of the individuals you will be working with. A due diligence review of the actual project will reduce the possibility of you unknowingly investing in an EB-5 project that is not a good fit for your needs and that will not meet the EB-5 requirements or be financially successful. As an investor, you should hire trusted EB-5 professionals to aid you in conducting a due diligence review, including your immigration attorney and possibly even an investment adviser.

When conducting a due diligence review of an EB-5 project, you should examine the project from an investment risk perspective with your investment adviser and from an immigration risk perspective with your immigration attorney. The EB-5 program has a lot of moving pieces, and no one person is an expert in everything, so it is smart to have an idea of who you should approach with each of your questions. This will help you avoid wasted time and frustration.

Investment Risk

You can hire an investment adviser to help you evaluate the project's finances. Some investors hire investment advisers to review a few different projects so that they can select an EB-5 project from a list of projects. Others hire investment advisers to help them find EB-5 projects that fit their personal interests. Either way, this person will help you understand the investment risks of an EB-5 project, particularly the likelihood that you will receive your investment capital back after the immigration process is completed. Part of reducing your investment risk, as previously discussed, is getting to know the project principals (the most important people in the project)—they make the financial projections for the project, which can significantly impact how your investment capital is used by the project and whether you will see your money again. Immigration may be your first goal, but EB-5 investments represent a lot of money at risk, and it is important to properly consider the financial aspects, especially because a project that fails financially is more likely to harm your immigration objectives.

Regional Center SEC Compliance. The US Securities and Exchange Commission (SEC) is the governmental agency in charge of protecting investors and making sure that the investment market is operating legally and fairly. Securities laws are designed to protect investors from fraud and encourage full and fair disclosure. Regional centers or projects must comply with certain laws when they are marketing investments to investors overseas—these laws prohibit anyone from misleading you or misrepresenting your investment. It is important to note that USCIS does not oversee regional center compliance with securities laws, so you may want to work with your investment adviser in this matter. As part of their licensing, investment advisers are required to assess projects in terms of SEC compliance, so having a third-party investment adviser analyze the regional center and its EB-5 projects will help increase the likelihood of your financial success in EB-5. If a regional center is not complying with securities laws, it can cause the developer significant and expensive problems that may make it difficult for the developer to complete the project. For example, the developer may be caught up in SEC enforcement proceedings that require funds committed to the project to be diverted to legal defense. Other investors in the project may have a right to demand return of their investments (plus significant interest well in excess of the EB-5 investment return) if the project was sold out of compliance with securities laws. When those funds are paid, the funds of remaining investors are in jeopardy. Moreover, if the regional center and developer are ignoring securities laws, you should ask yourself (and the developer) what other corners they may be cutting. Fortunately, if you discover during your due diligence review that the regional center or project is not following securities laws, you do not have to invest in its EB-5 projects.

Capital Stack. When considering an EB-5 project, you should consider your position in the capital stack. The offering documents should provide this information so you can review it with your immigration attorney or investment adviser. Knowing your position may affect your chances of having all or some of your investment returned to you when the project is complete. The capital stack is a common and important factor to consider when choosing an EB-5 project. The capital stack is the total amount of capital invested from different sources of funding (i.e., EB-5 capital, bank financing, and other funding) that has been pooled together to fund the project. Structurally speaking, different sources of funding will be placed in different positions of priority for security interests in various assets, distributions from cash flow, return of capital invested, and investment returns on capital. In project finance, the safest capital—the capital with first payment priority and the most senior liens on the most important collateral—is considered the base of the capital stack. The riskiest capital is considered the top of the capital stack. Different positions in the capital stack offer different levels of investment (and immigration) security. While EB-5 capital is usually pooled together in the capital stack as a group, individual EB-5 investors will be able to claim job creation according to any reasonable approach, such as starting with the EB-5 investor who files an I-526 first (i.e., the first investor to file his or her I-526 will claim the first 10 jobs, the second investor to file his or her I-526 will claim the next 10 jobs, and so on, until no more jobs can be claimed by EB-5 investors). Being the last EB-5 investor to a project may be problematic for job creation purposes, but that is why knowing that the project has prepared for unforeseen circumstances in its job predictions is so important. Be sure to discuss such issues with your immigration attorney before deciding what the immigration risks are with respect to such projects, including timing issues).

Projects that put EB-5 investments in the first (or senior) position for security on assets and priority on distributions are preferred from a capital stack perspective because you have first priority for receiving back any form of capital whether the project fails or succeeds. However, projects offering a first lien to EB-5 investors may have no other third-party capital (and sometimes no other capital at all), and that can be a risk factor. Projects that place EB-5 capital in the second or third position or EB-5 projects that lack any collateral protection will be riskier than first lien investments. Projects with a reputable bank holding a first lien are often financially stronger and have benefited from the due diligence review of such financial institutions. Such institutions have generally underwritten their own distributions and repayments, but senior lender due diligence usually also includes some confidence that the project will be able to pay its other obligations, including junior lenders and requirements payments to equity investors. In short, the position of EB-5 investors in the capital stack is extremely important, but such positioning must be considered along with other investment factors in order to provide a meaningful indicator of project risk. This is a complicated area requiring industry knowledge of the particular type of project. You should obtain the advice of an investment professional who understands project financing.

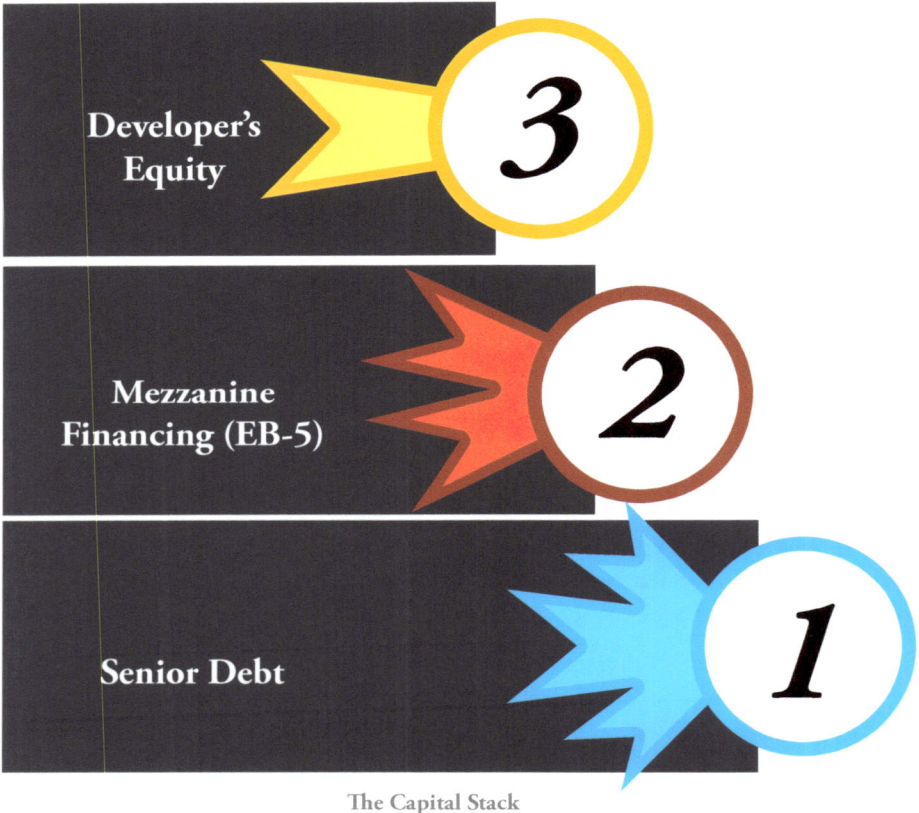

The Capital Stack

Exit Strategy and Return of Funds. Part of your due diligence review of a project's finances (with the help of your immigration attorney or investment adviser) is finding out whether the project has a clear and viable exit strategy for your investment. The exit strategy determines how and when you will get your money back after the immigration process is complete. Your position in the capital stack is factored into this. Generally, an EB-5 project's exit strategy is structured to begin approximately five years after your investment starts because that is the average amount of time that it takes investors to become permanent residents and no longer be subject to the "at risk" requirement for the EB-5 investment. For investments structured as a loan to the project, the loan will have a maturity date, which is the date that the project is required to pay back the fund in which the EB-5 investors hold interests (at which time such fund will normally liquidate and distribute funds to its investors). For investments structured as equity, the mechanism for repayment may be less clear and should be investigated in due diligence.

Regardless of the repayment mechanism, there will be no repayment unless the developer has liquid funds to pay you back. You, therefore, must consider the developer's strategy for producing these funds. The following are the common methods developers use to produce funds for an exit

- **internally generated funds:** These are profits from operations that can be used to repay investors. Very few projects will produce sufficient profits from operations in a five year timeframe to repay investors, particularly after considering the taxes that will be owed on profits earned. The developer may be required to place after-tax profits in a "sinking fund" to be used for investor repayment. The sinking fund will seldom produce enough funds to repay the investment by itself, but it can reduce risk by lowering the amount of funds needed from other sources to repay investors.

- **refinance**: EB-5 capital may be refinanced through a new loan or new equity investment. Sometimes, but not always, EB-5 capital will be refinanced along with a senior loan on the project. The ability for the developer to refinance will depend heavily on the economic success of the project (i.e., did the project meet or exceed its project projections, and what are the prospects for the future periods after refinance?). The ability to refinance will also depend on the overall health of United States capital and real estate markets. During the financial meltdown of 2008, it was difficult to refinance even successful projects. You should keep in mind that funds to refinance an EB-5 investment will likely be more expensive for the developer, meaning that the project must be performing very well in order to produce enough cash to meet the higher costs of the replacement capital.

- **sale of project:** The developer may sell the project to produce enough capital to pay lenders and investors. The funds produced from a sale will follow the distribution order of the capital stack. If the sale proceeds are insufficient to pay back lenders (and investors lower in the capital stack than EB-5 investors) EB-5 investors will lose their investment. Like refinance, the ability of the developer to produce an exit through sale will depend on the success of the project, and the health of capital and real estate markets for the asset type. The amount that buyers will pay for an income stream from a project can vary significantly, depending on economic conditions and real estate and other markets. It is very difficult (some would say impossible) to predict these cycles, especially five years in advance.

- **going public:** EB-5 capital is usually used for project finance, and projects seldom "go public" through public offerings. Even operating, growing businesses have a low likelihood of going public (though of course it does happen). You should treat any claim that an EB-5 project will repay your investment through a public offering with skepticism.

Owner Equity. Another thing to consider is how committed the regional center or developer is to the project. One way to measure this is to look at the equity that these players have committed to the project. If the regional center and/or project developer has not invested their own equity into the project, this should be a red flag to you that their financial incentives are simply to maximize their profits while leaving virtually all risk of loss on you and other EB-5 investors in the project (and possibly banks or others who either invest in the project or loan money to it). It may be a perfectly good project, but you may find your rate of return is too low for the amount of risk you are taking on by investing in this project. Ultimately, your primary focus as an EB-5 investor is making an investment in a successful EB-5 project, and when regional center or project developers do not invest in their own projects, they may be profiting excessively on your risk.

Bank Financing. In addition to knowing whether regional centers and developers invest in their own projects, you should know if the project has bank financing. If there is bank financing, it may mean that a US financial institution successfully performed a full due diligence review of the investment and that it was approved by the credit committee of a federally regulated financial institution. Banks loan money to businesses all the time and have experience knowing what will make a project succeed or fail. If a bank loans money to a business, they usually have good reason to believe that they will get that money back plus interest. On the other hand, you are strongly encouraged to ask additional questions of projects that purport to have bank financing. Most important, you should determine whether the bank has already committed to loan to the project and under what conditions. In some cases, the regional center or developer will say that a certain percentage of the project will be covered by a bank loan but then not actually have a firm commitment from the bank to lend. Also, take a look at the important terms of the bank loan, including interest rate, maturity date, collateral requirements (including subordination requirements for EB-5 financing), and important financial and operating covenants, which should be disclosed in the offering documents, with associated risk factors. Your immigration attorney or investment adviser can help you review these documents to determine whether the bank financing is just a regional center expectation or a true commitment from the bank itself.

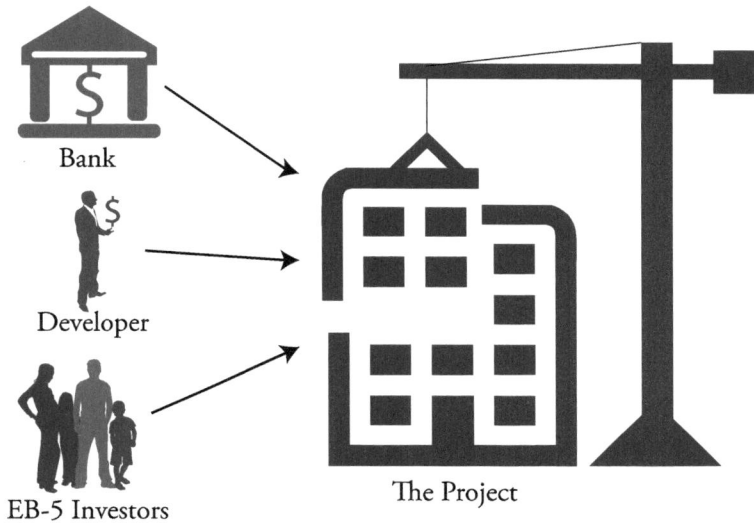

Bank

Developer

EB-5 Investors

The Project

Immigration Risk

Because EB-5 is both an investment program and an immigration program, you need to ensure that the project is as safe as possible from a financial perspective and from an immigration perspective. Specifically, you want to ensure that the project you choose to invest in will use your investment in a way that will fulfill the requirements of the EB-5 program and lead to a green card. Most importantly, will it comply with EB-5 regulations set forth by US government agencies and will the entity create at least 10 jobs from your investment? Due diligence is not complete without the review of your immigration attorney. Hiring an immigration attorney with substantial experience in EB-5 cases (EB-5 cases are much different from other, more general immigration cases) is important to your immigration success because this person will need to competently help you evaluate EB-5 projects from an immigration standpoint. As discussed in Chapter 1, your immigration attorney should be very knowledgeable in EB-5 and have a track record of EB-5 cases successfully completed. There are a number of critical legal questions that your immigration attorney should look into to determine your immigration risk, including:

- Does the EB-5 project you are investing in appear to comply with all relevant USCIS regulations?
- Does it seem likely that the EB-5 project will create enough jobs?
- Is the developer counting indirect jobs towards the number of job created?
- Is there a job buffer? In other words, are there a sufficient number of "extra" jobs projected—just in case the actual inputs into the economist's economic model (e.g., construction expenditures and operation revenues) fall short of expectations?
- How will you prove the number of jobs created when you file your I-829?

Answering these questions is important to your immigration due diligence review, and not being able to answer some of these questions to your immigration attorney's satisfaction could mean that the project may not be a good fit for EB-5 investment (even if it might otherwise be a fantastic financial investment). Additionally, when completing a due diligence review with your immigration attorney, you may find the following checklist helpful to guide your review. This process should take about two weeks to complete. The checklist includes typical due diligence items to review, all of which an immigration attorney sufficiently experienced in EB-5 cases will be familiar with and will be able to help you in reviewing:

Due Diligence Checklist:

- EB-5 regional center USCIS designation letter
- Regional Center Memorandum of Understanding (if the project developer is "renting" the regional center's EB-5 designation)
- TEA USCIS designation letter (if applicable)
- review of regional center compliance with SEC (i.e., not USCIS) regulations
- business plan
- independent appraisal
- government support on any level
- EB-5 history of all parties involved (e.g., the regional center, the developer, the contractor, the architect, and the immigration attorney and EB-5 economist who advised them)
- offering memorandum
  - limited partnership agreement, LLC operating agreement, etc., whichever is applicable

- subscription agreement
- escrow agreement
- visit to the project site and/or the regional center
- construction budget, schedule, permits, etc.
- term sheets and/or commitments
- project renderings
- operating budget
- economic impact report

(This checklist is not an exhaustive list. Consult your immigration attorney for the due diligence items that are most appropriate to your situation.)

If the project's documentation is complete, you will be able to review most of the information. In some cases, timing does not allow some information to be available, such as construction-related items like building permits, as work on the project may not be started at the time of your investment.

Offering Memorandum. The most important document for you to review with your immigration attorney is the offering memorandum, or the private placement memorandum. This document describes the project's goals, the terms of the investment, and the risks associated with the investment. The offering memorandum will contain a complete summary of three documents:

- the limited partnership agreement, LLC operating agreement, etc. (whichever is applicable)—this document outlines what your relationship to the business will be and lists everyone's rights, obligations, and responsibilities.

- the subscription agreement—this document is basically an agreement from the project to sell you ownership interests and for you to pay for them.

- the escrow agreement (if applicable)—this document describes the conditions under which your investment funds will be released to the project. There is a whole range of approaches. Some projects do not use escrow at all; they just transfer your funds directly to the project as soon as you invest. Other projects escrow your funds only briefly until they accept your subscription agreement (which is practically the same as no escrow). Other projects release some of your funds right away (e.g., $400,000) and then the rest (e.g., $100,000) upon approval of your I-526 petition. Yet other projects hold the entire $500,000 until your I-526 petition is approved. Because they all differ, your immigration attorney and you need to review the escrow terms carefully so that you know exactly when your funds will be released to the project.

Offering Memorandum

The offering memorandum will sometimes include the business plan as well. The offering memorandum summarizes the significant terms of these documents, but is not a replacement for reading them. Collectively, the offering memorandum and these documents are referred to as the "offering documents." As part of the due diligence process, after you review the offering documents, you can follow up with any questions you may have about the project and its offering documents with the regional center or project developer. If you do not understand the information that has been provided—or if the regional center is unwilling or unable to provide the information—you should not commit to the EB-5 project until your questions or concerns are answered. There are a lot of EB-5 projects out there, and more are created all the time, so it is okay to wait for one that seems right for you.

At this point, you may be asking yourself, *Do I need to pay someone to translate these documents so that I can review them in my own language?* The answer to that question is somewhat complicated. The bottom line is that you should definitely understand the documents and what they mean for your financial and immigration future. The question is how to best achieve that. Even though some regional centers translate the offering documents for their investors, you still need to ensure that you understand what they mean. Even if you hire a third-party translator to verify the accuracy of the documents, that still does not necessarily mean that you will sufficiently understand the content. For example, even native-born English-speaking Americans frequently hire corporate or securities attorneys to review such offering documents before investing in similar projects.

If English is not your native language, you are likely at a double disadvantage because you may have difficulty with the language, and also may not understand how business practices work in the United States—even if you are an expert in business practices in your home country. Sometimes, you can find US attorneys who speak your language fluently, but to be effective (and to be more than merely a translator), they have to understand the underlying law very well, and it can be very difficult to find lawyers with such capabilities. Again, whether you rely on a translator, a team comprising a native-English speaking lawyer with expertise in the technical information and a qualified translator, or a bilingual lawyer, you need to find a way to ensure that you understand the documentation and what it means for you and your family's financial and immigration goals.

Regional centers are not required to provide you with translated copies of the offering documents; however, if they do, the translated copy is legally required to be accurate and contain the same information provided in the originals. If you find that your translated copies do not match up with the originals, you may have the right to seek legal action to recover your investment at any time. Speak with your immigration attorney if you find yourself in this situation— your immigration attorney will be able to support you during this process or direct you to appropriate counsel.

Job Buffer. When conducting a due diligence review of the project's economic impact report, you will learn how much of a job buffer your project offers its investors. EB-5 investments are no different from any business ventures in this respect—economic conditions and public demand for the project's goods or services can change, construction can be delayed, or expenses may add up more quickly than anticipated. For this reason, it is important to verify that whatever project you are investing in is creating more than the required number of jobs to protect you in case anything unexpected should occur—in the EB-5 industry, this is commonly called a job buffer.

Tip

As an EB-5 investor, you should consider job creation your first concern on the *immigration* due diligence review. After all, failure to create the necessary number of jobs will prevent you and your family members from receiving your green cards.

Generally speaking, a *buffer* is something that offers protection, so a *job buffer* protects you, the investor, from the possibility that a project will not create the required number of jobs you need to receive your green card. When regional centers or projects determine the maximum number of EB-5 investors to accept for a project, most factor in a job buffer of at least 20 percent of the jobs in the economist report, to account for any projected jobs that USCIS may not accept or that may not be created as a result of things not going as planned. This means that good EB-5 projects with a job buffer will plan to create more jobs than the investors are required to create based on the number of investors involved. For example, the economist may calculate that a project will create 100 jobs, but will proceed in accepting investors as though they expect only 80 jobs to be created.

Tip

"Safer" projects do not accept the maximum number of investors that could be accommodated based on the economist report because they want to ensure that the investors they do accept will be able to meet the job creation requirement. The economic report that the economist creates is only an estimate of the jobs that will be created, so having a firm understanding of a project's job buffer will help protect you against the possibility that the project will not create the 10 jobs each investor will need. A job buffer of 20 percent implies that the project accepts investors that will claim only 80 percent of the total jobs in the projected in the economist report.

Consider this example: a hotel project wants to raise $10 million for a project under an EB-5 regional center. To raise this $10 million in funding, the project needs 20 investors, each investing $500,000 and each needing to create 10 jobs for a grand total of 200 jobs needed for the project. This hotel project could theoretically accept 20 investors if it obtains an economist report showing 200 total jobs created. However, a prudent developer of this hotel project should be more conservative in terms of job creation and allow for a job buffer. If the well-prepared economist report shows only 200 jobs will be created, this project may accept only 16 investors in order to maintain a 20 percent job buffer (160 jobs is 80 percent of 200). Thus, the hotel project would lower its EB-5 raise to $8 million as opposed to $10 million and maintain a 20 percent job buffer.

Big Projects vs. Small Projects. The overall size of an EB-5 project is not the most important factor in determining either immigration or investment safety. The most straightforward way to assess the immigration safety of the project is to look at the job buffer—in general, the higher the job buffer, the safer the job-creation aspect of the project. In addition, one must consider how the job creation is predicted. Specifically, you should review with your immigration lawyer, not only how large the job buffer is, but also which components are used in the job creation numbers. For example, job creation based on tenant occupancy and visitor expenditures may be relatively more risky than job creation based on construction or general operations. You and your immigration lawyer can find the job buffer in the economic impact report, which you can obtain from your regional center. Review this document with your immigration lawyer to determine whether the job buffer is sufficient for your needs as an EB-5 investor.

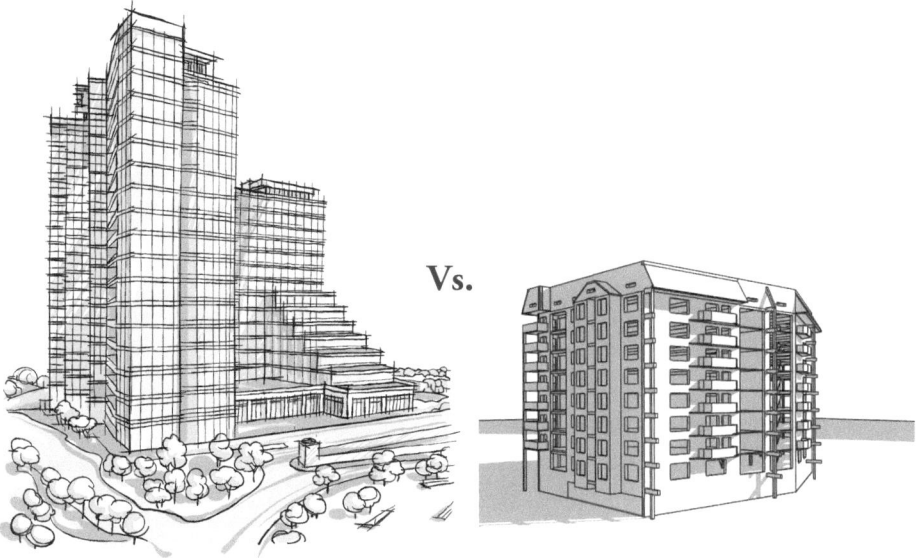

Vs.

OUTCOME SCENARIOS

Ultimately, all EB-5 projects are different, and the success of an EB-5 project can be measured in both immigration terms and investment terms. Of course, your goal is to receive your green card and have your funds returned, but this is not always the case, which is why it is critical for you and your immigration attorney and any other advisers to help you determine how risky your investment is from both perspectives. There are four outcomes that can result from EB-5 projects:

Outcome Scenarios

1 A good project will have the highest likelihood to make enough money and create enough jobs to return your investment and qualify you for immigration.

Some projects will be successful enough to return all of your money, but not create enough jobs for you to obtain your permanent green card—or the project otherwise turns out to violate one or more of the various EB-5 requirements. For example, this could happen if your EB-5 capital is invested successfully (from a financial perspective), but not the way the business plan said it would. Or it could be that the funds were properly invested, but USCIS changed its rules part-way through the process. This risk has been reduced since USCIS adopted a "deference" policy, indicating that it recognizes that policy changes should apply only to future cases rather than cases already in progress.

If the project successfully creates the required number of jobs, but fails to return funds to its investors because the business didn't make enough money, you and your family members could still get your green cards, but you may lose part or all of your investment. For this reason, it is important to understand not only the general financial risks of the business itself, but also your position in the capital stack (because your position will determine whether you will be paid back if there is not enough money to return capital to all investors).

This is the worst outcome because you will not receive your green card or money back. You can reduce the chance that this will occur by conducting a thorough due diligence review before investing in an EB-5 project. Fortunately, as the EB-5 industry continues to grow, you (and other EB-5 investors) will likely find it easier to become more informed when evaluating projects.

FAILURE TO COMPLETE DUE DILIGENCE

Occasionally, regional center operators, developers, or agents accidentally or intentionally engage in marketing or operational approaches that could put your family's investment and green card dreams at serious risk. In other instances, one or more levels of the overall process engage in fraud, attempting to trick not only the investors, but others whom you may interact with along the way. For example, some might even try to advertise fraudulent EB-5 projects or pretend to operate under so-called regional centers that do not have valid USCIS designations. Such problems are worst case scenarios in EB-5, but due diligence is important not only to detect fraud but also to evaluate risks that exist in every EB-5 project.

Two major scandals that highlight the importance of due diligence in EB-5 are A Chicago Convention Center (ACCC) and USA Now Regional Center. Knowing about them can help you learn from others' mistakes.

A Chicago Convention Center

In 2013, according to the SEC, project developers at ACCC used false and misleading information to get funding from EB-5 investors. During the investigation, the SEC said that these developers collected more than $11 million in administrative fees from more than 250 Chinese investors who were trying to participate in the EB-5 visa program. The SEC alleged that the ACCC developers lied about when construction would start and what parts of the project had already been completed and that when investors gave them money, they spent it before they were supposed to do so. The SEC caught wind of the scandal before all of the investors' capital had been collected and brought charges against these individuals in an attempt to prevent the Chinese EB-5 investors from losing even more money. Unfortunately, the entire situation could have been avoided had the investors' migration agents conducted even the most basic analysis of the EB-5 project. On the positive side, the ACCC scandal has since caused migration agents everywhere to work harder on due diligence for the projects they advertise. Overall, most migration agents serve their clients well and play a positive role in the EB-5 program, but there are certainly low-quality migration agents who place their clients into bad projects without engaging in sufficient due diligence of the overall EB-5 offering, including the principals leading the project. This scandal is a reminder of the importance for you, the investor, to conduct a thorough due diligence review of all parties you work with. Moreover, as an investor, it is your responsibility to know who your migration agent is and his or her track record with EB-5 investors. Remember that, while rare, there are fraudulent EB-5 projects out there trying to get your money. If something seems wrong or too good to be true, take a closer look.

USA Now Regional Center

The ACCC scandal is just one example that draws attention to the importance of due diligence. With any EB-5 project, you should always be cautious before committing to the project, which means looking at all aspects of the project. For example, if you don't complete a due diligence review of the regional center you plan on working with, you may find yourself in a similar situation to the EB-5 investors who failed to review USA Now Regional Center. In 2013, the SEC brought charges against USA Now Regional Center for dealing with investors before USCIS had even designated it as a regional center. In addition to not having USCIS designation, USA Now Regional Center allegedly misused EB-5 capital for personal gain by building a restaurant while promising their EB-5 investors that their capital would remain safe in escrow until USCIS approved the regional center. As a result of EB-5 capital going towards the wrong EB-5 project, these investors did not receive their green cards. Like the ACCC scandal, this case highlights the importance of thoroughly evaluating and considering all aspects of a potential EB-5 project from both an immigration and an investment perspective while also getting to know all of the players involved in the project.

Due Diligence Questions to Ask Yourself:

1. Is my migration agent experienced in EB-5 cases? How is my migration agent being paid?

2. Is my immigration attorney experienced in EB-5 cases? Is my immigration attorney getting money from any other parties in the EB-5 program? Does my immigration attorney have my immigration goals in mind, or is this person more interested in making money from my investment?

3. Is the regional center designated by USCIS? Has the regional center conducted its own due diligence review of the project?

4. Does the business plan show that the number of jobs I need will be created? Does my investment adviser agree?

5. Does my translated version of the project offering documents contain the same information as the original documents I received from the regional center?

CONCLUSION

Due diligence is critical to your success in the EB-5 visa program. Conducting a thorough due diligence review helps increase the chances that the individuals you are working with are experienced in EB-5 and are competent and careful with your immigration and investment needs. As the investor, you need to get to know each person you plan on working with. You need to have your immigration attorney and other advisers carefully and objectively review the project documentation and other information to lower the chances that you won't get your green card or your money back.

Also, when looking to hire immigration attorneys, migration agents, and investment advisers, make sure these individuals tell you how they are being paid and who else may be paying them so that you can make sure there are no conflicts of interest that could risk your immigration success. Hiring the right team of advisers whom you can trust is very important to your success in the EB-5 program. These individuals will help you review projects, regional centers, and how they plan to use your money so that you are more likely to receive your green card and get your money back at the end of the process.

When conducting a due diligence review of regional centers and their projects, work with the team of EB-5 professional you have hired (e.g., your immigration attorney and your investment adviser) to make sure you are asking the right questions. This team is there to help you through the investment and immigration process and make sure you are setting yourself up for investment and immigration success. In particular, it is important that everyone on your due diligence team has sufficient expertise in EB-5 to help you navigate through the different steps of the EB-5 visa program.

CHAPTER 4: HOW DO I APPLY FOR MY VISA?

By David Hirson and Linda Lau

Now that you have found an EB-5 project and conducted a thorough due diligence review of your project and the players involved, it is time for you to actually make your investment and begin the visa application process. Getting a green card through the EB-5 program is a multi-step process that typically can take about four to five years to complete, so count on your immigration attorney to help you every step of the way!

After the end of this five-year process, hopefully you will have your investment returned to you, depending on the project's exit strategy and what terms you agreed to when you committed. Investors typically participate in EB-5 for the immigration benefits and are most concerned about getting green cards for themselves, their spouses, and their unmarried children under 21 years of age. Their primary goal is for their families to experience the benefits of permanent residency (which are described in this chapter) and, for many, to educate their children in the United States. Once USCIS grants you and your family members' green cards, you will have the option to become naturalized citizens of the United States.

This chapter will give you the information you need to help you achieve your immigration goals and know what to expect during the visa application process.

Generally speaking, immigration to the United States is a very detailed, technical process, and getting your green card through the EB-5 visa program is no exception. But don't let the technical nature of applying for your green card steer you away from EB-5—for most EB-5 investors, the immigration benefits are well worth the wait. And you will not be alone in this process: your immigration attorney is hired for the purpose of submitting all of your paperwork to USCIS so that you have the best chances of receiving your green card.

This chapter is intended to give you an overview of the process so that you can be better informed when working with your attorney. Your immigration attorney will help you complete every step of this process and remind you of important deadlines. Don't be intimidated by the details, or think that you need to memorize the steps—this chapter is merely informational so that you will become a more informed EB-5 investor with a higher chance of success.

TRANSFERRING TO THE ESCROW ACCOUNT

As mentioned earlier, most EB-5 investments are made by transferring money into escrow accounts that are associated with the project. (Remember, in EB-5, an escrow account is a third-party US or foreign bank account that holds onto your money until it can be released to the EB-5 project). Transferring your investment to an escrow account can help to protect your investment in the case that your I-526 is denied and you want to have your money returned to you quickly. (As mentioned in *Chapter 3*, however, there is a broad range of escrow arrangements, so be sure to ask your immigration attorney to review the escrow terms carefully for you so that you understand what the arrangement is for your particular case.)

Ideally, projects and regional centers are supposed to structure financing in ways to try to ensure that your money is the most effective at creating jobs. Your immigration attorney or regional center can explain to you the financing structure of your project and answer any questions you may have.

Tip

Your regional center and/or project developer will give you the information you need to transfer your money. This step is very important because you must have committed some (or the full amount, depending on the escrow agreement you signed with the regional center) of your investment to the project before your visa application will be approved.

Navigating Currency Restrictions

Depending on where you are from, transferring your investment can be moderately difficult. However, EB-5 investors have been successfully transferring funds since the inception of the program. If you have concerns about such transfer-related issues, most immigration lawyers with substantial experience working with EB-5 investors can either answer your questions or refer you to a specialist with technical knowledge.

Beginning the Application Process

After you have committed your investment to the project, your immigration attorney will help you prepare and file Form I-526 with USCIS, which presents evidence to show USCIS how you are meeting the requirements of the EB-5 visa program. Because your I-526 petition is a very important step to receiving your green card, this chapter will explain the visa application process and other requirements and what your immigration attorney will be doing to help you reach your immigration objectives.

THE EB-5 VISA APPLICATION PROCESS

Getting a green card through the EB-5 program is a three-step process that typically can take about four to five years to complete. This sounds like a long time, but you can typically expect to move to the United States before the entire process is over. You must wait for USCIS to approve each form before you can move to the next step.

1. File Form I-526 (Immigrant Petition by Alien Entrepreneur) to show your eligibility for the conditional permanent resident visa. This form will include evidence that you are actually in the process of investing, and include documents from your project showing how your investment will meet the job creation requirements of the program.

2. File either Form DS-260 (Immigrant Visa Electronic Application) if you are outside of the United States when filing or file Form I-485 (Application to Register Permanent Residence or Adjust Status) if you are inside the United States in a valid nonimmigrant status, such as a student visa, work visa, etc., when filing. Upon approval of whichever application you file, you will either travel to the United States to start your two-year conditional green card status (if you filed a DS-260) or you will automatically start your two-year conditional green card status (if you filed an I-485, your two-year conditional green card status will automatically start upon the approval of your I-485 application).

3. File Form I-829 (Petition by Entrepreneur to Remove Conditions) to become a permanent resident without conditions. (You will file this during the 90-day window before your two-year conditional green card period expires.)

Tip

Timing for Chinese Investors: If you were born in mainland China and if the EB-5 category "retrogresses" in the future, you may experience a delay of perhaps a year or possibly longer between the time your I-526 petition is approved—(you can always file your I-526 petition even with retrogression)—and when you are eligible to immigrate to the United States. You don't need to know all of the technicalities of retrogression, but if you were born in mainland China, you need to be aware of the issue and ask your immigration lawyer about it to help understand the issue and what it might mean for you and your family, especially children who are approaching 21 years of age.)

Understanding the Steps

Before getting into the technical details that your immigration attorney will be responsible for, you need to have a general understanding of what each step means for you so that you are familiar with the general process and know that your immigration attorney is staying on track with filing the necessary paperwork with USCIS or a US consulate in your home country.

Step 1: Form I-526. When your immigration attorney files Form I-526, this shows USCIS how you are eligible for the EB-5 program. Approval of this form does not automatically give you a visa. To receive your conditional permanent resident visa (the one you need to immigrate to the United States), you still need to complete the next step of the process.

Step 2: Consular Processing (DS-260) or Adjustment of Status (I-485). You will complete Step 2 by applying for your two-year conditional green card at a US consulate in your home country (through a DS-260 application) or applying for your two-year conditional green card via a process known as "adjustment of status" in the United States (through an I-485 application).

Step 3: Form I-829. When your immigration attorney files Form I-829, this shows USCIS how you met all of the requirements of the EB-5 program. Approval of this form removes the conditions from your two-year conditional green card status and converts it to a permanent green card status.

STEP 1 DETAILS: FILE FORM I-526

A lot of detailed work goes into preparing and filing your Form I-526 for USCIS to review. Below is some general guidance on what you and your immigration attorney will be doing to prepare and file your I-526 petition. (In later sections, we also explain the details of the subsequent forms and documents you and your immigration attorney will need to file to move you through the entire process toward your permanent green card through EB-5.)

Preparing Form I-526

As mentioned above, your I-526 petition must present evidence to USCIS of your investment and how your investment is expected to create at least 10 jobs for US workers. In addition to helping you prepare the form itself, your immigration attorney will also help you decide what supporting material will need to be provided for USCIS to review. (Examples of documents are discussed below.)

The Supporting Documents. In general, the supporting documents comprise two different sets of information. One set shows that you obtained your EB-5 investment funds "lawfully" and that you transferred it to the new commercial enterprise for your EB-5 investment. The other set shows what the new commercial enterprise you invested in plans to do with your investment funds and how the regional center economist believes your investment will create at least 10 jobs for US workers. You do not need to know the details of each of these documents (your immigration attorney will help you with the technical aspects of the application), but you should be generally familiar with what documentation is required so that you can start thinking about how you will be able to obtain or prepare the documents your immigration lawyer will need to prepare and file your case.

EB-5 Requirement	Supporting Documentation
You have invested in a qualifying project or business	• limited partnership agreement, LLC operating agreement, articles of incorporation, or similar entity-formation documents as well as state certificates showing that the entity is duly registered in the state of formation • certificate of merger or consolidation (if applicable) • business license • subscription agreement • other entity-related documentation
You have invested or are in the process of investing $500,000 (or $1 million, if applicable)	• bank statements, wire transfer receipts, etc. • evidence of funds transferred in exchange for ownership interest in the new commercial enterprise • invoices, sales receipts, and purchase contracts (normally only applicable if you are investing in a direct investment project instead of in a regional center project)
Your money was acquired lawfully	• personal and business tax returns filed anywhere in the world in the last five years • foreign business registration records • certified copies of all pending cases involving money judgments against you within the last 15 years • documents identifying any other lawful sources of money invested • loan or mortgage agreement (if you borrowed the funds you intend to use for your EB-5 investment) • any other documentation relevant to the lawfulness of your investment funds

Your business will create 10 fulltime US jobs	• "comprehensive" business plan showing when the required number of employees will be hired within the next two years • economist job-creation report showing that the pro forma numbers in the business plan will, when run through a reasonable economic model, create at least 10 jobs for US workers • copies of tax records and employee I-9s (if you have already created some jobs—normally only in a direct EB-5 petition)
You are in a management position in the business	• statement of your title and a description of your duties (if applicable) • evidence that you are a corporate officer or hold a seat on the board of directors, or that you are engaged in management or policy-making decisions

Filing Your I-526

You should receive a receipt in the mail that your application was received by USCIS. This receipt has an application receipt number you can use to track your application status on the USCIS website, or you can ask your immigration attorney about the status of your application.

Request for Evidence (RFE). While USCIS is reviewing your application, they may ask you for more information or evidence if something appears to be missing from your petition. This is called a Request for Evidence (RFE). Even if USCIS issues an RFE, that does not mean that your case will be denied; it just means that USCIS has some questions, so don't get discouraged if this happens to you. Your immigration attorney can help you determine what evidence USCIS is looking for and how best to present that evidence in a way that will make it more likely that USCIS understands how you meet the EB-5 requirements.

The Consular Visa Interview (If Applicable). The focus of the consular interview is more on you as a person than your EB-5 project, but you still need to be at least somewhat familiar with your I-526 and your EB-5 project in case the consular officer asks questions about them. For the most part, the interview will focus on whether the documents and information you provided to USCIS or the consulate are true. Normally, if that information and documentation are true and accurate, you should have nothing to worry about at the consular interview. Nonetheless, you need to know enough about the EB-5 project to help the officer understand that you are capable of serving in at least a non-binding advisory role at the company. Typically though, the bulk of most interviews is more about your personal life—the relationships with your family members, any criminal record, your reasons for moving to the United States, etc.

You may be denied entry into the United States if you:

- have committed certain crimes
- have certain diseases
- don't seem to have relationships with the family members you claim to have (for example, you claim to be married, but don't have a marriage certificate with you)
- have extreme political views that could be dangerous (i.e., the officer feels that you may engage in terrorism)
- have previously broken immigration laws in the United States
- seem to have lied or misrepresented anything on your application

Typically, your immigration attorney will help you prepare for your interview. Of course, if you are worried about any particular issue in your case, you should discuss that with your attorney very early on. In particular, when your immigration attorney asks you about any criminal issues, communist party membership, etc., at the very beginning of your case, it is safest to answer truthfully, as your attorney cannot help you as well without the facts. In many cases, problems can be resolved before your interview, but if the facts are not discovered until you actually arrive at the interview, the officer could make it extremely difficult and time-consuming for you to obtain your EB-5 visa.

The I-526 Decision

If your I-526 is *approved*, your immigration attorney will help you complete one or the other of the "Step 2" options mentioned above (i.e., obtaining your green card through a DS-260 consular processing application or an I-485 adjustment of status application).

If your I-526 is *denied*, your immigration attorney can discuss options with you, such as appealing your case or filing a new I-526 with USCIS. In some appeal cases, it may actually be faster to file a new I-526. In any event, your immigration attorney can help you decide the best course of action under the circumstances. Also, if USCIS denies your I-526, it will tell you why, which will help your immigration attorney know what to do to try to make a stronger case next time.

Processing Time. You should normally expect to wait at least 9–12 months for your I-526 to be processed—sometimes more, sometimes less.

Fee. The current filing fee for an I-526 petition is $1,500. You can pay this amount with a check or money order payable to the US Department of Homeland Security.

STEP 2 DETAILS: CONSULAR PROCESSING ADJUSTMENT OF STATUS

Like Step 1, your immigration attorney will help you complete Step 2. Step 2 actually has two different options. The one that you will use depends on where you live when you need to complete this step. The Step 2 options are called "consular processing" or "adjustment of status."

Option A: Adjustment of Status

If you live within the United States under a temporary visa (such as F-1 student visa or H-1B work visa), your immigration attorney can adjust your status within the United States from that temporary visa status to a conditional permanent resident by filing Form I-485.

Preparing Form I-485

You won't be alone in preparing and filing this form, so don't worry— your immigration attorney will help you the whole way. Like the I-526, your immigration attorney will attach certain documents for USCIS to review before it will adjust your status to conditional permanent residency. For the I-485, USCIS will primarily be interested in your personal history because USCIS has already reviewed the EB-5 project itself when it reviewed your I-526 petition. With your I-485, your immigration attorney will include the following documents, some of which you may need to help collect for your immigration attorney:

- criminal history (if applicable)

- family certificates (e.g., birth certificates, marriage certificates, and divorce or annulment papers, if applicable)
- copy of passport page with nonimmigrant visa (if you are residing in the United States under another visa)
- two passport-style color photos
- fingerprinting (this is called biometrics services by USCIS)
- police clearances
- medical examination
- some basic biographic information about you and your family
- a copy of your I-526 approval

Filing Your I-485. Like the I-526, your immigration attorney will file all of this paperwork with USCIS. If USCIS feels like something is missing from your form, or if they need more information about you before making a final decision, it will issue you a "Request for Additional Evidence" (commonly called an RFE). In some instances, it will ask for an interview.

The I-485 Decision. If USCIS approves your I-485, you will have conditional permanent residence for two years. This means that you can live within the United States for the next two years. But your residency is conditional, so you will be living in the United States conditionally. The condition is that your EB-5 project creates the number of jobs you said it would in your I-526. If the project you invested in doesn't create the jobs at the end of the two years, you will not receive permanent residency, and you will not be able to stay in the United States.

Also, during this two-year period, you must show that you plan on making the United States your home. You can show this by filing tax returns in the United States, educating your children in US schools, or any other action that would show USCIS that you plan to permanently live in the United States. However, this two-year period can be troublesome for some EB-5 investors who may want to visit their home country for long periods of time.

Tip

If you want to travel abroad for six months or more during this time, even if it is just for business, you must apply for a travel document/re-entry permit by submitting documentation with USCIS before you travel. If you do not take this step, you may have to convince an immigration judge that you really are planning on living in the United States. If the judge thinks that you are not acting like a permanent resident, you will lose your conditional resident status. You will be seen as having "abandoned" your residency in the United States.

Processing Time. It can take 3–4 months for your I-485 to be approved and your status to be adjusted, sometimes longer. During this time you will retain your conditional permanent residency status.

Fee. The current filing fee is $985, plus an $85 fingerprinting fee, for a total of $1,070. Like the I-526, you can pay this amount with a check or money order payable to the US Department of Homeland Security.

Option B: Consular Processing

If you live in your home country when it is time to complete this step, you will need to complete consular processing to receive your conditional permanent resident visa. Your immigration attorney will help you prepare for this visit, although he or she will not physically be present at the US consulate to help you.

Applying for Your Two-Year Immigrant Visa through Consular Processing

As mentioned above, there is also another option to apply for your green card after USCIS approves your I-526 petition. If you are living in your home country when your I-526 is approved, you will apply for your immigrant visa at a US consulate or US embassy in your home country. Getting your immigrant visa through consular processing requires the same documents that you would need for an I-485 petition, but you just apply through different procedures. Your immigration attorney will help you prepare for your visit to the consulate. Once your I-526 is approved, USCIS will notify the National Visa Center (NVC). The NVC will then send you instructions and appointment packages and will request the same documents asked for in the I-485.

The Consular Processing Decision. Like I-485 approvals, if you are approved during consular processing, you will be able to come to the United States for your two-year period of conditional permanent residence. You don't have to enter the United States immediately, but you (and your family members) must enter the United States within six months after the consulate approves your immigrant visa.

Processing Time. It currently takes about 3–12 months to complete consular processing. This timeframe varies from country to country, though, and can change. When you get to this step, ask your immigration attorney whether there are any updates to this general estimated timeframe.

Fee. You will need to pay processing fees along the way for the consular process, but typically you should budget about $500 per family member. Your immigration attorney will let you know the exact amount when you get to this step.

STEP 3 DETAILS: FILE FORM I-829

Filing your I-829 is the final step you need to complete to receive your permanent green card. If approved, you can permanently live and work in the United States without any conditions (but this does not make you a US citizen). Your immigration attorney will help you file this form 90 days before the end of your two year conditional permanent residency. By the time you file your I-829 petition, you will have lived in the United States for about two years, and your EB-5 project should be wrapping up and coming to a close.

Preparing Form I-829. Essentially, your I-829 tells USCIS that you did everything you said you would in your I-526. Instead of giving USCIS documents that show what you will do, your immigration attorney will give USCIS documents showing what you did do. If approved, this form removes the conditions on your visa. Just like the other steps, your immigration attorney will work with your regional center to gather the documentation needed for this form. With your I-829, your immigration attorney will provide USCIS with the following documents, some of which you will need to give to your immigration attorney, but you will know which items you are responsible for by the time you reach this point:

- a copy of your permanent resident card (Form I-551)
- any criminal history (since becoming a permanent resident)
- supporting documentation showing how you met the requirements of the EB-5 program

The chart below has some common supporting documentation you normally will be expected to provide to USCIS to prove how you met EB-5 requirements.

EB-5 Requirement	Supporting Documentation
You invested in a qualifying project or business	• federal tax returns
You invested $500,000 (or $1 million) in the business.	• financial statements

You sustained the investment during your two-year conditional residency.	• invoices and receipts • bank statements • contracts • business licenses • federal or state income tax returns or quarterly tax statements
Your business created at least 10 full-time US jobs	• payroll records • relevant tax documents • employee I-9s • (If you invested in a regional center-based EB-5 project, you will need to provide the documentation that the regional center provides to your immigration attorney, which will typically focus on expenditures instead of employee-specific information.)

As you can see, many of the supporting documents are the same as those you filed with your I-526. This is because your I-526 tells USCIS how you intend to meet the EB-5 requirements, and your I-829 tells USCIS how you actually met those very same requirements.

Tip

This is why your due diligence review of your regional center becomes especially important—the number of jobs you report to USCIS must match the number of jobs estimated in the regional center's business plan. If you created enough jobs but did not create them in the way the business plan said, you will not receive your green card.

Filing Your I-829. To file your I-829, your immigration attorney will mail your form to the appropriate USCIS facility as listed on their website.

Like your other forms, USCIS may ask you for more information or evidence. They may also ask to interview you. Be prepared, but don't be panicked—this happens from time to time.

The I-829 Decision. Approximately four to five years after making your investment, you will finally know whether or not you will become a permanent resident! While your I-829 is being processed, you are still a conditional permanent resident. Your status will be extended until your I-829 is approved (or denied). If your I-829 is approved, congratulations! Approval of the I-829 officially makes you a permanent resident of the United States.

However, if your application is denied, USCIS does not think your investment meets the requirements of the EB-5 program, and you will be asked to leave the country. Unfortunately, there is no appeal for a denial at the I-829 stage. If your I-829 petition is denied, you should talk with your immigration attorney about what to do next. Most commonly, your choice will be to leave or try to get an immigration judge to approve your I-829.

Processing Time. You should expect to wait 6–12 months, but this can sometimes be much longer.

Fee. The current filing fee is $3,750, plus an $85 fingerprinting fee (for you and your family members) for a total of at least $3,835. You can pay this amount with a check or money order payable to the US Department of Homeland Security.

After your I-829 is approved, you have finally reached the point in the EB-5 process when your investment can be returned to you. For more information about when you will have your funds returned, you should refer to the project's exit strategy. See Chapter 3 for a more detailed discussion of typical exit strategies for EB-5 projects.

CITIZENSHIP (NATURALIZATION)

If USCIS approves your I-829, this does not make you a US citizen. If you wish to become a US citizen, you must go through the naturalization process. US citizens can vote in elections and do not have to worry about being deported (certain crimes will result in removal from the country even if you are a permanent resident). But you may not want US citizenship for a few of reasons (e.g., your native country may not allow dual citizenship, which would mean that you will lose citizenship in your home country if you become a US citizen, or other factors). But if you do want to become a citizen, you must follow the naturalization process. In order to qualify for citizenship through naturalization, you must:

- have been a permanent resident for at least five years
- physically be in the United States for at least 30 months out of those five years
- be 18 years old or older
- be able to read, write, and speak English and understand basic US history and government
- be a person with good moral character and support the Constitution of the United States

Although US citizenship is beyond the scope of this EB-5 book, the general outline is provided here in case that is part of your overall planning. The table below outlines similarities and differences between US lawful permanent resident status and US citizenship.

Right/Responsibility	Permanent Residency	US Citizenship
Live permanently in the United States	Yes (as long as you do not commit certain crimes)	Yes
Work anywhere in the United States	Yes	Yes
Be protected by and required to obey all laws	Yes	Yes
Leave and return to United States	Yes	Yes
Go to public schools and colleges with in-state tuition	Yes	Yes
Join the military	Yes	Yes
Vote	No	Yes
Qualify for social services	No	Yes
Have a US passport	No	Yes
Pay taxes	Yes	Yes
Report to Jury Duty	No	Yes

FREQUENTLY ASKED EB-5 QUESTIONS

When can I move to the United States?

You can move to the United States after you complete your consular visa interview during the "consular processing" mentioned above in "Step 2" and you enter the United States using that immigrant visa. (If you instead file for "adjustment of status" while in the United States, USCIS will convert your status without you needing to leave the United States.) At this time, you will have conditional permanent residency, which is a legal status for living and working in the United States.

What happens if my current visa expires while I wait for I-526 approval?

If your current visa expires while you wait for I-526 approval, you may run into serious complications, so you need to plan your overall immigration strategy with your immigration attorney in advance. For example, if you remain in the United States after your temporary visa status expires, you may be prevented from returning to the United States in any status for three years or more.

To keep this from happening, you should be careful not to let your current visa expire. There are ways to do this. For example, you can apply for your current visa to be extended so that it will still be valid when you have your I-526 approved. Again, you should talk to your immigration attorney about your options and plan early on in the process so that you don't run into any unexpected problems.

Can an illegal immigrant apply for the EB-5 program?

Unfortunately, if you entered the United States without authorization or if you overstayed a nonimmigrant status (e.g., student visa or work visa), you normally cannot apply for a green card through the EB-5 program. If these circumstances apply to you, you should definitely consult an immigration attorney in advance to see what other alternatives you might have for obtaining a green card.

What are the most common reasons for the denial of an I-526 petition?

One common reason that I-526 petitions are denied is that the petitioner didn't have enough evidence that all the money was earned lawfully. This is why it's important to have an immigration attorney who has experience working with EB-5 law, especially for petitioners from your country of origin.

Another common reason is not quite proving that you'll be able to create enough jobs with your investment. Again, this is why you should plan to work with an experienced team of EB-5 professionals at each step of your effort to obtain a green card through the EB-5 petition and application process.

How is the application process different from other visas?

Many investors choose the EB-5 program because of the opportunities that US residence and citizenship can offer their families, particularly education for their children. Investors want their children to be able to study in the United States as soon as possible, but they are also looking for long-term opportunities through successful immigration. Given these objectives, families may mistakenly believe that applying for investment immigration is as simple as applying to study abroad—first find a project/school, then simply provide relevant information as needed. For this reason, many families will appoint the non-working spouse—who may have little or no concept of how to handle business operations or investment analysis—to apply for investment immigration, rather than the businessperson in the family. Although, as you have learned, the EB-5 program is quite user-friendly when working with the appropriate professionals, it is important to understand the intricacies of the application process before getting started.

When investors approach the EB-5 program in the same way that they would approach an application for a student visa, they run the risk of overlooking important aspects that may affect their green card success. While you may select a school based on rankings, personal fit, and even the beauty of the campus, selecting an investment project requires a more careful analysis of the immigration requirements and the likelihood that the project will be financially successful. When investors select a project as if they were selecting a school they run the risk of: 1) analyzing the project from a *noncommercial* point of view, 2) relying too much on the advice of family and friends, and 3) falling under the spell of an unqualified migration agency's hospitality and marketing with no real understanding of the project. Before starting the EB-5 immigration process, be sure that your whole family understands the requirements of the program and the level of analysis necessary.

How do I avoid bad projects?

In order for your immigration application to succeed you need to choose a project that will succeed. The situations below are real world examples of what you should look out for when selecting a project.

The Project Developer Has No Track Record. It's not a hard fast rule; however, the project you choose should have an experienced developer leading the charge. Like many other aspects in life, choosing someone with a track record is a smart practice. A developer with past experience, for example, in the development of hotels, assisted living, or commercial development has most likely endured the growing pains and learned job-specific business lessons that are invaluable. When choosing a project, making sure that the developer has a track record of success will at least satisfy a general concern of whether the developer can pull off the project. Many projects require licensing, permits and entitlements, and the developer with experience will have an easier time navigating governmental hurdles.

Other Sources of Financing for Selected Project Are Unclear. For nearly all EB-5 investment projects, the source of funding consists of the EB-5 investments, sponsor equity and for some, commercial loans. If any portion of the financing encounters problems, the entire project may be affected. Make sure you are working with the appropriate EB-5 professionals to conduct due diligence and understand all levels of your chosen project's financing.

The Selected Project Has Faced Financial Difficulties. Some projects you consider may have run into funding difficulties prior to EB-5 financing, and may be attempting to reverse their problems through new EB-5 financing.

However, many of these projects end in failure, as there are usually good reasons why a project has been denied funding in the past. If a project goes bankrupt, it may be difficult or near impossible to recover your investment amount. Be wary of projects that have demonstrated previous failures.

Be sure to carefully select the project that you will invest in—do not fail at the starting line. Avoid: 1) projects operated by inexperienced developers; 2) projects in which other sources of funding are absent or unclear; and 3) projects that faced financial difficulties. In order to avoid these mistakes, you can hire experienced professionals to evaluate your selection, personally obtain more information from the project for a better understanding, and where necessary, conduct site visits and get a feel for the state of the project, first-hand.

CONCLUSION

The EB-5 approach to obtaining a green card is the perfect fit for certain investors, and if that's you, then you can become a permanent resident of the United States! It can be a complicated process, though, and you will need to work with your immigration attorney and regional center (or project developer) to gather all of the documents you need for each step of the overall process. We wish you best of luck with your case!

PART II

Guide for the Developer

INTRODUCTION
by Ali Jahangiri

The EB-5 visa program was started to create American jobs and fund US economic development. Established in 1990, the program offers green cards to foreign investors in exchange for a job-creating investment in a US enterprise, but it also offers extraordinary benefits to you, the developer. The low-cost capital alternative (often situated in the capital stack like mezzanine debt) that EB-5 investments provide has become increasingly popular, especially in the wake of the recent economic crisis. Regional centers—you'll learn more about that term later—have popped up around the country to facilitate EB-5 projects and foreign investor capital has funded many high-profile projects. The program is a win-win-win: developers can raise capital at a lower cost, investors receive a coveted US green card, and the general American public benefits from job creation and GDP growth. Here is some basic information about the program that you'll need to understand before we discuss in more detail the considerations of whether EB-5 capital is right for your project and, if so, how to make it work for your goals.

WHAT IS AN EB-5 VISA?

An EB-5 visa allows foreign investors the opportunity to come to the United States as permanent residents (green card holders), provided they meet certain requirements:

- make an "at risk" investment of $500,000[1] or $1 million, depending on where the business project is located in the United States
- create (or in very limited circumstances, preserve) 10 jobs for US workers through their investment

The process requires coordination among a network of qualified professionals to ensure that investors and developers are meeting all the requirements of the program, but the basic requirements really are that simple. If you would like to know more about the visa and investment requirements on the investor side, you can read Part I for a detailed analysis. For developer purposes, however, Part II will cover all you need to know to get started in the program.

1. Congress has for a number of years considered changes to various parts of the Immigration and Nationality Act (INA), which includes the EB-5 program, so it is possible that if and when Congress changes the INA, Congress may also include changes to these minimum investment amounts for the EB-5 program, resulting in an increase of the minimum investment.

Tip

You probably noticed that the first bullet point stated that investors can make a $500,000 or $1 million investment, based on where the investment is located. Investors will qualify for the lesser amount ($500,000) if the project they are investing in is located in a targeted employment area (TEA). A targeted employment area is defined as a rural area or an area experiencing unemployment of at least 150 percent of the national average. Because TEA projects allow investors to invest only $500,000, most EB-5 projects are located in TEAs.

THE DEVELOPER'S ROLE

As a developer, you play an important role in the EB-5 process by providing a project that will accept an investor's funds and serve as the basis of their EB-5 application. To do this, you will likely work with a regional center (or maybe decide to start one yourself), which is a public or private entity that focuses on job creation, economic growth, and capital investment in the United States—and is designated by the US government. Regional centers facilitate EB-5 investments and enable projects to raise more money as a result of enhanced job counting available only through projects sponsored by a regional center. Good regional centers will work with a team that provides a full scope of EB-5 services. This team will include immigration attorneys, securities/corporate attorneys, economists, business plan writers, and possibly broker-dealers. The agency that is in charge of the EB-5 program—including the designation of regional centers—is United States Citizenship and Immigration Services (USCIS). This agency will come up again and again throughout *The EB-5 Handbook* and while you are working within the EB-5 industry.

As you will learn in Part II, EB-5 investors' main goal is to secure US green cards for themselves and their families. Secondarily, they are looking to receive their original investment amount back as soon as possible after the visa process is complete. As a developer in the EB-5 program, satisfying these investor goals are among your primary obligations. Unlike regular investors, immigrant investors are usually not looking for market returns on investment—returns to EB-5 investors (which must be distinguished from your total cost of capital) are usually in the range of 0.5 to 2 percent. The real returns on their investments are the visas they intend to receive. Because of this, you will need to pay close attention to following USCIS guidelines so that investors (and your project) will meet all of the requirements of the program.

HOW TO USE PART II—GUIDE FOR THE DEVELOPER

Part II is a general guide for the developers looking to raise capital for a project. The topics explored here are set up to reflect the logical ordering of questions you will ask about the program. By the end of *The EB-5 Handbook*, you will know who to work with and how to get started raising EB-5 capital for your project or business.

Chapter 5: Is EB-5 Right for My Project?

Chapter 5 will help you understand the EB-5 program in greater depth and understand how EB-5 capital is different from other, "traditional" sources of capital. Through a hypothetical example of a development company considering EB-5, you will see many of the important questions that developers should ask of the program before they get started. Chapter 5 presents an extensive list of factors to consider when determining if EB-5 is right for your project.

Chapter 6: What Makes a Successful EB-5 Project?

As you have already discovered, the EB-5 program requires the developer to meet certain goals. Because of this, just because a project is financially successful does not necessarily mean that it will be a success in EB-5 terms. Chapter 6 will help you understand success in EB-5 terms by explaining your responsibilities as a developer and what investors will expect of you. You will learn the importance of assembling a proper team, marketing your project, meeting job creation requirements, and returning investor funds.

Chapter 7: How Should I Use EB-5 in the Capital Stack?

By the time you reach Chapter 7, you will have a grasp of the program and what a successful project looks like. Part of project planning is determining if EB-5 investment fits in your capital stack. Chapter 7 will discuss how your capital stack can affect the marketability of your project and how it plays into job creation considerations. You will learn about the two main EB-5 capital structures—the loan model and the equity model, as well as bridge capital and certain program regulations that affect EB-5 in your capital stack.

Chapter 8: What Are My Regional Center Options?

In order to raise EB-5 capital, you will likely work with an existing EB-5 regional center, or create one of your own. This chapter will go deeper into the regional center concept and present the options you have for working with one. Chapter 8 will also outline the difference between regional center and nonregional center (direct) investments. After introducing the concepts, Chapter 8 delves into creating your own regional center or affiliating with an existing one. By the end of this chapter, you will be aware of the alternatives, becoming more educated before consulting with your attorney.

Chapter 9: How Do I Raise EB-5 Capital?

And now, the big question: How do I obtain EB-5 capital? This chapter will discuss using escrow to accept investor funds and how this affects investor and project outcomes. Before you can sell-EB-5 securities for your project, you must prepare a package of offering documents. Chapter 9 will identify the documents commonly included, and set your expectations for timing and cost. Chapter 9 also talks marketing strategy and practicalities, and how to work with migration agents in China—the EB-5 program's largest market for investors. The chapter ends with a discussion of securities compliance and other important legal considerations that all developers must keep in mind when operating within the EB-5 field.

Chapter 10: What Are My Responsibilities After the Capital Raise?

As developers, you already know that the work is not over when you have successfully raised capital; it is just beginning. Chapter 10 focuses on fund administration, or how to use investor funds in an appropriate way to meet your financial goals and their immigration goals. Beyond that, Chapter 10 discusses EB-5 considerations for your exit strategy and how funds are typically returned to investors.

Chapter 11: The Future of EB-5

Throughout *The EB-5 Handbook*, you will get a sense of the impressive growth of the EB-5 program and its movement towards becoming a more mainstream financing mechanism. Chapter 11 will take stock of how far the program has come and the challenges it has confronted along the way, and predict where it will go from here. It includes discussions of recent administrative changes and proposed legislation that would reform and improve the program for developers. This chapter contextualizes the program in a wider economic and political context, and gives you a glimpse of the questions that the EB-5 community of stakeholders considers on a daily basis.

CHAPTER 5: IS EB-5 RIGHT FOR MY PROJECT?

By Dawn Lurie and John Tishler

Chapters 1-4 delved into the details of the EB-5 visa program and investor requirements. Those chapters focused on EB-5 from the investor's perspective.

In chapters 5-11, we switch gears to look at EB-5 from the perspective of the U.S. developer, covering all key aspects of EB-5 as project capital, including: whether EB-5 is appropriate for your proposed project (Chapter 5), what it takes to create a successful EB-5 project (Chapter 6), how best to use EB-5 funding in your capital stack (Chapter 7), what options you have available for creating or "affiliating with" a regional center (Chapter 8), how to go about raising EB-5 capital (Chapter 9), how to comply with all applicable laws after the capital raise and eventually return the capital to your investors (Chapter 10), and the future of the EB-5 program (Chapter 11).

Determining if EB-5 is appropriate for your project requires an understanding of how EB-5 capital works in the real world. This chapter explains how raising EB-5 capital differs from obtaining capital from other sources. In particular, this chapter focuses on factors to consider when trying to determine whether EB-5 funding is likely to be a good match for your project.

EB-5 CAPITAL VS. TRADITIONAL FINANCING

There are pros and cons to using EB-5 capital to fund your project—EB-5 capital is not right for every project. To determine if your project is an appropriate fit for EB-5 capital, you need to consider a number of factors that may influence your decision.

Factors to Consider

- cost of capital
- availability of capital
- financing terms
- leverage
- recourse
- timing and planning
- up-front transaction costs
- management diversion
- securities law liability

This chapter will use Crown Development, a hypothetical developer, to explore some of these factors and help you digest this information.

Crown Development owns three acres in a secondary urban market. Crown Development purchased the land during the economic downturn for $1.5 million and estimates it to now be worth $5 million. Its team has done all of the preparation work for a 160-room, limited-service hotel under a well-known brand (or "flag," as it's known in the hotel industry). The property will have an outdoor swimming pool, 2,000 square feet of meeting space, a business center, a fitness center, a gift shop, and a dining area that serves complimentary hot breakfast to every guest. Construction costs are $200,000 per room key, or $32 million total. Crown Development owns the land outright and has arranged for a bank to lend 50 percent (or $16 million) of the construction costs on a first lien, no recourse basis. The bank is insisting that Crown Development invest at least $4 million of its own equity into construction. Crown Development can obtain the additional $12 million from several potential sources, including private investors interested in equity, an equity-based real estate fund, or a number of subordinated or mezzanine lenders. The hotel is anticipated to take 18 months to build.

Should Crown Development seek EB-5 capital for the additional $12 million it needs to fill its capital stack?

Cost of Capital. EB-5 capital is typically used for the portion of the capital stack that must be funded with mezzanine capital, traditional equity, or preferred equity. For these portions of the capital stack, EB-5 capital is dramatically cheaper to the developer as compared to other traditional mezzanine sources, which typically cost between 9 to 20 percent per year, often with points up front and/or equity participation in the project's upside. In today's EB-5 market, a developer can expect to pay a fixed rate between 5 percent to 8 percent per year, including amortization of all up-front costs, for use of EB-5 capital over a five-year expected investment horizon. The cost for this usually subordinated capital may be only slightly above today's prevailing bank rates (after purchasing a swap to fix the rate) for a first position loan on a high-quality project for a reputable developer funding perhaps 50 to 65 percent of the total construction costs.

If Crown Development can support the necessary job creation for its EB-5 investors (at least 10 jobs per EB-5 investor), which is typically easy for new hotel construction when less than half of the construction budget is EB-5, the cost of capital savings on $12 million over a five-year investment horizon will be extremely attractive.

Availability of Capital. Historically, EB-5 has been raised for projects that were unable to raise necessary capital from traditional sources. This is not the case today, as it is becoming more difficult to market weaker projects. This is due to the crowded market for EB-5 projects, particularly in China, the high profile failures of some EB-5 projects, and the increasing sophistication of investors and their advisors in underwriting projects. Nonetheless, demand for the EB-5 program is at an all-time high and investors are ready and willing to invest in quality projects.

Financing Terms. EB-5 investments tend to be "covenant lite." That is, the developer does not typically promise to maintain financial ratios, provide detailed reports—such as actual cost to budget or financial statements—or refrain from taking actions without consent of the investors. As discussed later in this book, the requirement that investors be active in management is typically satisfied by providing them with skeletal rights of a limited partner, and with these rights, investors typically have little or no power to direct management decisions other than participating in the formation of policy and voting on limited matters.

With the possible exception of equity from friends and family who invest purely on trust, EB-5 is the most favorable investment available to developers when it comes to freedom from covenants and investor management rights.

> By using EB-5 financing, Crown Development can benefit from reduced covenants and management rights compared to other forms of capital.

Leverage. EB-5 investments typically follow a "loan model" or are structured as an equity interest with debt characteristics. Using EB-5 capital can result in greater leverage for the equity investors in the project, who will rarely share appreciation in value with the EB-5 investors. Greater leverage means greater internal rate of return to the developer and the equity partners.

Normally, greater leverage also means more risk, but the risk of EB-5 leverage is mitigated by the low cost of capital and the covenant-lite nature of most EB-5 investments.

> Crown Development may be able to increase its own equity returns and the internal rate of return for equity partners by safely increasing leverage with EB-5 funds.

Recourse. EB-5 investors most often have recourse only against the project. They seldom have recourse against the developer's other assets and virtually never have personal guarantees. By the very nature of EB-5, investor capital must be "at risk", so the return of EB-5 investor funds cannot be guaranteed. (While uncommon, for regional center projects, USCIS-adjudication policy currently does allow a guarantee of the obligation of the project owner to repay the new commercial enterprise owned by EB-5 investors, as contrasted with a guarantee of repayment direct to the EB-5 investors.)

Timing and Planning. EB-5 capital takes a relatively long time to structure and raise, and usually even longer to become available to your project. This is largely due to EB-5 capital remaining in escrow until visa milestones are met. Time horizons of nine months to two years (and sometimes even longer) are common, depending on the type of program (i.e., whether it is a direct investment or regional center investment) and what model is used for regional center sponsorship in an indirect program.

For most developers, aligning the EB-5 timeline with the project's construction timeline is the biggest hurdle to overcome. The first thing you must consider is the time it takes to find EB-5 investors to subscribe to your project. Then, the investors must expatriate liquid funds and file paperwork with USCIS to apply for their visa (Form I-526). Funding and filing the I-526 petition may take a few months, and once investors submit the petition to USCIS, it will take many months until the application is approved. Though USCIS has taken steps to shorten the time for I-526 adjudication, at the time of this book's publication, adjudication has been running 12 to 18 months. Some projects wait until all I-526 applications are approved by the USCIS before releasing capital from the escrow account. The full process from launch of the offering to availability of funds can therefore run 15 to 24 months.

Some projects are structured to release some or all of the capital from escrow upon USCIS-approval of a certain number of I-526 petitions or even upon filing of I-526 petitions. This is referred to as "early-release," and you will learn more about this in Chapter 9. In almost any realistic situation, developers should expect longer wait times than other forms of capital, so timing and planning are major concerns when dealing with EB-5 capital.

Two options to mitigate such delays are bridge financing or self-funding during the waiting period for I-526 approval. USCIS will often permit EB-5 funds to "take out" other project funds, which can be critical to the feasibility of an EB-5 program to fund a project.

Crown Development does not need the EB-5 capital right away, as it has its own funds and bank senior debt funds that can fund those construction costs incurred while EB-5 capital is raised and investor petitions are approved by USCIS. Crown Development may also be able to bridge construction costs beyond its equity commitment and bank loan using its own funds or a commercial EB-5 bridge lender, pending a successful raise and release of funds from escrow. Of course, these bridge sources of capital will be more expensive than EB-5 capital while they are being used.

Up-Front Transaction Costs. Up-front costs are a major downside of EB-5 capital. Not only are the transaction costs higher than many other forms of capital, but many of them must be paid well in advance of receipt of capital to offset those costs.

It is important to note that most of the up-front transaction costs are relatively fixed and depend little on project size. Accordingly, up-front transaction costs are a bigger problem for smaller projects than they are for larger projects. You should model the amortization of realistic transactions costs to determine your true cost of EB-5 capital and the savings you will achieve over traditional forms of capital.

Crown Development will need to get comfortable with paying higher up-front transaction costs for EB-5 funds than for other available funds. The capital raise of $12 million is towards the lower end of the amount that justifies these up-front costs. However, Crown Development has sources of capital it can use to pay these up-front costs. Crown Development may recoup some of these costs through the administrative fee (see *Chapter 2* for a discussion of regional centers and administrative fees) or the spread between what investors are paid in annual return (usually less than 2 percent) and what the project is paying (usually 5 to 8 percent). Regional center projects with a strong likelihood of raising $10 million or more can usually justify the upfront costs.

Management Diversion. EB-5 is a complex industry and typically requires more human capital for raising EB-5 funds and navigating the details of the program. For this reason, some developers choose to outsource completely to industry insiders (or fundraisers) while others choose to take on the challenge and hire and supervise a good team. When raising capital, management normally must select and contract with professionals, participate in structuring the offering, participate in drafting the offering materials, and travel to countries where investors reside to market and promote the project.

Additionally, significant management attention is required during the life of the investment to assemble and disseminate the information that investors need to progress in the immigration process, attend to escrow release requirements, and communicate with a heterogeneous group of investors who may speak limited English.

Because the EB-5 process is so management-intensive, it is often easier for larger companies with a deeper management bench. This is true both when initially raising capital and during the life of the investment.

The amount of management diversion required of you depends on the relationship you and your project have with fundraisers. A full service fundraiser can make EB-5 much easier on the developer and significantly increase the odds of fundraising success. There are a number of companies that provide these services: some own the regional center and others contract with regional centers, but either way, they achieve the same end—running the process and raising EB-5 capital for your project.

Crown Development should engage knowledgeable EB-5 professionals to advise on the time, work, and travel commitments involved, and if it proceeds, Crown Development should ensure it has the necessary resources. Ideally, the professionals consulted will be willing to speak the truth about the amount of work involved, the amount of work they and others can and will do, and the true costs of outsourcing what Crown Development cannot or will not do itself. Crown Development should be careful about choosing professionals based on price alone. While many skilled EB-5 professionals will quote a low fixed or "not to exceed" price, they do so based on a limited scope of work. Obtaining limited scope of work quotes from professionals can leave major gaps in services that jeopardize funding success, strain the developer's personnel resources, and imperil the visas for investors. A professional that quotes a realistic price will typically represent the best overall value.

Securities Law Liability. Raising EB-5 capital involves a syndicated offering of securities. Securities laws in the United States and elsewhere create significant administrative and litigation liability exposure to developers.

Persons who participate in a flawed offering of securities can be found personally liable for investor losses. This aspect of securities law has the potential to take away the non-recourse advantages discussed above. It is also a crime to violate securities law, and people do go to jail for securities fraud.

The good news is that potential securities law liabilities are not difficult to mitigate. Firms have been raising money in syndicated project finance offerings to foreign investors for many decades, and the vast majority of these offerings do not result in civil or criminal liability. The key is to use the practices that have evolved over the decades to make offerings safe for you and your project. These practices include robust disclosure, using law firms with deep experience and substantial reputations in capital markets transactions of all kinds, and approaching the fundraising from a standpoint of compliance rather than a standpoint of looking for legal loopholes. These are the practices seen every day in international private offerings, and there is no good reason not to employ the same practices in EB-5 offerings.

<u>CONCLUSION</u>

EB-5 capital has unique characteristics that make it very attractive in certain cases and unattractive in other cases. Advance planning is key to evaluating and optimizing EB-5 in the capital stack. The best way to find out if EB-5 is right for your project is to speak with an EB-5 professional experienced in all manners of financing projects.

Assuming the job creation requirement is satisfied, Crown Development's project would seem to be a strong fit for EB-5 funding. The positive factors seem to outweigh the negative factors—most of which could be mitigated with skillful planning. Other projects with different characteristics may present a lower likelihood of success on important factors, including job creation and market acceptance, and therefore may be a less compelling fit for EB-5 than Crown Development's project.

CHAPTER 6: WHAT MAKES A SUCCESSFUL EB-5 PROJECT?

by Joe McCarthy and Kyle Walker

As a developer, your participation in the EB-5 visa program is more than just weighing the pros and cons of using EB-5 capital to fill your capital stack. To be able to attract EB-5 investors to your project, you will need to show investors how your project plans to be successful within the confines of the EB-5 program—namely, how it will create jobs. After all, investors will not subscribe to projects that will not help them meet their immigration objectives, because green cards are the primary reason that investors participate in EB-5. The more easily you can show that your project will meet EB-5 requirements, the better your chances of raising EB-5 capital.

The majority of investors invest through EB-5 regional centers, and successful regional centers are built from successful projects. There are currently around 500 USCIS-designated regional centers and this number is quickly growing. The majority of these regional centers are not active. As USCIS's understanding of applicable EB-5 law, regional economics, securities laws, real estate development, and real estate finance continues to improve, the application process for obtaining USCIS designation for an EB-5 regional center has continued to become substantively more reasonable and procedurally more streamlined. There are, however, significant barriers to succeeding as an EB-5 regional center after receiving USCIS designation, and by extension, there are significant barriers to promoting and developing successful EB-5 projects.

DEFINING SUCCESS

So what creates successful projects by EB-5 standards? What do EB-5 investors mean when they say, "I want to invest through a successful EB-5 regional center?" You will likely get a range of answers from investors, but they are most likely looking for three factors that determine a regional center's successful track record, and these factors largely relate to successfully passing visa milestones with USCIS:

1. I-526 adjudication success
2. I-829 adjudication success

3. return of investor capital

Regional centers that can share how they have met these three factors are considered successful by EB-5 standards. Successful regional centers not only help their investors meet EB-5 visa requirements, but they also work with projects that they perceive to have a high probability of returning capital to the investor at the end of the EB-5 process. Truly successful regional centers will be able to show a proven track record of accomplishing investor goals—investors like to see that regional centers consistently work with successful EB-5 projects. Repeated success, especially with I-526 and I-829 approvals, lets investors know that they are in good hands and will be working with a regional center that knows how to operate in the EB-5 world.

Though long track records boost investor confidence, even regional centers that are doing everything right may have trouble showcasing this. Because it takes about five to seven years to return capital to investors, and syndicated EB-5 offerings under regional center sponsorship are still relatively new, only a few regional centers have actually been around long enough to return capital to investors. The majority of regional centers are currently operating within that five to seven year window and simply do not have figures of success to share with investors yet. As the program continues to grow and gain momentum, more and more regional centers will be able to share their success of returning capital to investors. In the meantime, focus on success at each of the key stages of the process. The key to regional center success is developing successful EB-5 projects, and successful EB-5 projects begin with a knowledgeable team of experts and professionals.

Recipe for Success: Your Team

Whether you choose to operate a regional center that will support multiple EB-5 projects, or you are just looking to use EB-5 for a single project, forming a team of experts in their respective fields is the best way to set up a project for success in EB-5. Your team should be highly experienced at what they do, starting with you, the developer. The developer should have a long track record of project success. In addition to that, you need the right team of EB-5 service providers. Every developer's situation is different, so you will need to determine the proper course of action for you and your project. If you are a developer just getting into EB-5, you can outsource the EB-5 process partially or completely. Hiring a team can be as simple as hiring a third party to take care of everything EB-5, or you can "do-it-yourself," which often involves working through, or "affiliating with," an existing regional center. You have many options for assembling your EB-5 team, all of which should be determined by your particular project, experience, and EB-5 comfort level: some developers manage their own EB-5 capital raises, some use EB-5 regional centers to manage the entire EB-5 process, some use consultants who handle portions of the process, and some use different combinations of these players. Whichever direction you choose to go, you should hire your team based on experience and successful track records, skill and personal compatibility.

If you decide to do it yourself, either by starting your own regional center or affiliating with an existing one, you will be hiring a team of service providers. Because EB-5 law is relatively complex and because legal counsel is necessary to produce a successful offering, your team should include, at a minimum, an immigration attorney, a securities/corporate attorney, an EB-5 economist, and an EB-5-experienced business plan writer. To complete your team of service providers, and to facilitate the actual capital raise, you will also find a regional center to affiliate with (or end up filing for one yourself) and hire an international team to promote your project, which would include migration agents and consultants. In contrast, if you contract with a third party with EB-5 experience, they probably have their trusted network already in place. Chapter 8 will help you decide which option is the best for you and your project.

The Project: Financial Viability and Marketability

An EB-5 project needs to be both financially viable and marketable to be successful. Most projects that are financially viable have a good chance of being marketable, but not all marketable projects have a good chance of being financially viable. There have been many projects in recent memory that were very financially sound but did not have great stories to tell to attract investors. Funding a residential apartment complex in Brooklyn, NY may provide a very safe investment for EB-5 investors, but if it is not marketed in an enticing or appealing way, it may not draw much interest or EB-5 funding. On the other hand, there have been many projects that are visually appealing and glamorous, but poorly underwritten. Once EB-5 investors look beneath the surface—and today you should count on them doing just that— they will discover that such projects have little substance and are unlikely to be successful. Combining financial viability and marketability is the key to "selling" your project abroad and raising investor funds.

Meeting EB-5 Requirements: Job Creation

The two main priorities for any EB-5 investor are the security of their family's green cards and the security of their $500,000 or $1 million investment. First and foremost, the project needs to be able to create the requisite number of jobs to secure green cards for each investor, and the project cannot be considered a success otherwise. Each project has its own unique job creation analysis—no two projects are alike. There are multiple economic methodologies that an economist may use to establish the job count for your project, including RIMS II, IMPLAN, REDYN, or others. Another factor that will affect the total job count is the location of the project. Economic forecasting software programs take into account the cost of labor and income level of the project's particular locale. For example, a project in Dallas, TX may create a different amount of jobs than would an otherwise identical project in Boston, MA.

In addition, both USCIS and investors will want to see some extra jobs created by the project to serve as a "buffer" in case the expected inputs in the economic model come up short of expectations. Such a buffer will help to ensure that even with a drop in inputs the remaining amount of input (be it revenue or expenditures or some other category) will still be enough to cover the job-creation requirements of all of the EB-5 investors in the project. While a shortfall of one or two jobs may not seem like much in the context of a large project, it only takes one missing job to jeopardize an investor's green card. The marketplace will demand that you have an adequate job buffer.

Aligning the EB-5 Timeline with Your Project's Timeline

Let's assume you have a financially viable and marketable project and you have a business model that safely projects creating the required number of jobs. The most challenging part of achieving success, which was briefly touched upon in the previous chapter, is aligning the EB-5 funding timeline with the actual project timeline. It is critical not to underestimate the amount of time it may take for the capital to be raised and then to be released from escrow, which typically hinges on approval of the I-526 or, in other cases, the issuance of the EB-5 investors' immigrant visas. If you miscalculate, your project may stall or you may be forced to find other, more expensive, capital as an alternative, while you wait out the delivery of EB-5 funds. Developers typically wait 8-18 months from the initial term sheet to actual availability of capital for project investment. This timeframe varies depending on the size of the capital raise, the marketability of the project, and the terms of escrow release.

Tip

It typically takes 1–2 months for your own due diligence and term sheets, another 1–2 months to prepare investor-related documents, such as the private placement memorandum, and 1–2 months to actively get into the international market (and this is assuming you already have some level of status internationally and a capable team of agents who have previously marketed your projects). After a few months of fundraising, EB-5 investors need to begin filing I-526 petitions, which can take 2-3 months after subscribing, and then the petitions often have to be approved before funds are released from escrow (unless there is early-release), which can take 12-18 months.

When and how funds are released from escrow may differ from project to project. Some regional centers use escrow in the strictest fashion and do not fund until their investors have I-526 approvals. This poses quite a bit of risk directly to the project and indirectly to the investors, as a 12-month or more processing timeline is difficult to factor into a construction schedule, but nonetheless, some regional centers adhere to this. Other regional centers will release a portion of the investment dollars once they have a certain number of I-526 approvals. It all depends on the situation. There are even few who do not use an escrow: the funds are wired straight to the project (or limited partnership that then funds the project). Aligning this funding timeline with the development timeline is probably the single most challenging aspect to EB-5. The task is not impossible, however—understanding processing timelines and matching your expectations with the reality of EB-5 funding will help you plan a project calendar that aligns with the availability of capital.

Returning Investors' Funds

In addition to feeling secure about meeting immigration objectives, the likelihood of receiving back the $500,000 (or $1 million) investment is of obvious importance to EB-5 investors. As such, a very clear exit strategy needs to be in place to attract investors—without any guarantee or redemption—so that the investor understands the path for exiting the project and having their capital returned. Most exits are scheduled for about five to seven years after the initial investment, assuming a two-year construction timeframe. Construction loans, which are prevalent in almost every real estate project, EB-5 or not, also typically last five years, which is why it is easy to align the EB-5 term in this fashion.

For most real estate projects, exits will be either a sale of the underlying asset or a refinance of the asset (See Chapter 3). Some projects sell additional parcels or lots, and some EB-5 investments are traditional equity opportunities and require a much longer hold time before the investor can exit. Regardless, the project should be underwritten by real estate professionals to ensure that there is a viable exit— regardless of its length—that will result in the return of the investors' capital. A strong exit strategy that outlines how and when investors will be repaid is a huge factor that investors will consider when choosing a project.

TAKING THE FIRST STEPS

Now that you know what it takes to develop a successful EB-5 project, it is time to take the first steps. As a developer you will need to choose whether to outsource the capital raise process entirely or to do some of it yourself. If you choose to outsource, many of the following steps will be taken care of for you, provided you choose an experienced team. If you choose to work with your team to raise the capital yourself, you will need to pay attention to some key practicalities.

Regional Center Designation/Affiliation

Obtaining USCIS designation of your regional center or affiliating with an existing regional center will get you, as the project developer, on your way toward your effort to raise EB-5 funds. USCIS designation or shared services arrangements, however, are just the first steps and Chapter 8 will walk you through these. The main challenge will be setting up your project to appeal to migration agents and potential investors.

Marketing the Project

Let's assume you have successfully structured the perfect EB-5 project. You are projecting jobs above and beyond the requirements, there is a clear exit strategy to repay the investors in full, and you have even managed to align the timelines so that you are reasonably confident that you will be able to fund the project when the construction timeline calls for it. Now, how are you going to market it?

Marketing projects is much more complicated if you are offering your project to investors from 40+ countries as opposed to, say, China only. Culture comes into play in EB-5, as certain investors see benefits in different types of projects based on their background and their nationalities. Some investors like larger projects with indirect-only construction jobs; others like the certainty of full-time direct jobs, such as in senior housing projects; and others look at location first and foremost, especially with real estate projects, and job creation is an afterthought (as long as visa requirements are met). Staffing your company with a diverse team— employees who have lived abroad—can enhance your chances of structuring an offering that will be well received across all continents. A mistake that many regional centers make is setting up unnecessary local offices around the world—in Shanghai, in Dubai, etc.—incurring significant overhead of questionable value.

Location. Obviously, project location is critical to the project's financial success, but it is also important when marketing to potential EB-5 investors overseas. If your location is a strong selling point, it helps to lead with that. Also, it is important to understand that for cultural and other reasons, many EB-5 investors (especially those from China) seem to strongly prefer investing in major U.S. markets, such as New York, Los Angeles, Chicago, Houston, and so on. Therefore, if your project is not in one of these major markets it is important to highlight other underlying advantages of your project's location that perhaps a larger market may not have.

Appeal. Prestige sells. It is no less true in EB-5. Many high-net worth foreign investors are used to the high life, and because they are going to choose one (and only one) EB-5 project, many are going to choose something that makes them proud. Enlisting the help of a design team to produce videos, brochures, graphics, and other attractive marketing materials can help to promote your project. An architectural firm will likely have already been hired to produce renderings, and, as long as they present the project favorably, you should consider using them in the promotion of the project.

EB-5 in the Capital Stack. Regarding the capital stack, there have been many successful projects with the EB-5 investors in the first position, mezzanine position, or equity position—there doesn't seem to be a correlation of success with position. However, many investors are encouraged when they see that the developer has contributed its own share of equity (be it cash equity or land equity) to the project. This encumbers the developer with a certain amount of financial risk, which differs from reputational risk, and investors seem to understand the difference. Land that is already owned seems to be an easier sell than land that needs to be bought, although both structures have succeeded in the EB-5 market.

EB-5 Trends and Policy Changes. It is also important to understand that as USCIS adjudication policy evolves, so do the particular attributes that make a project marketable, so stay up to date with EB-5 trends to increase your chances of success.

CONCLUSION

A successful project is the key to a successful capital raise. Your project can take many forms, and the way you subscribe investors can take many forms—either through a developer owned and operated regional center, or through a regional center that you affiliate your project with. Whatever the method, investors are looking for an offering backed by promoters that can demonstrate a strong record of success. Success in the eyes of investors means getting their green card and having their capital returned.

To build a successful EB-5 project, you will need to assemble a team of qualified professionals, learn how to structure your offering so that it will be financially viable and marketable, and ensure that you are meeting all the requirements of the EB-5 program so that investors will reach key visa milestones. In the next chapter of *The EB-5 Handbook* we will walk you through the next step, how to incorporate EB-5 into the capital stack of your offering.

CHAPTER 7: HOW SHOULD I USE EB-5 IN THE CAPITAL STACK?

By Linda Lau, Jeff Campion, and John Tishler

Much of what has been covered so far in this book focuses on understanding the EB-5 program, whether it is right for your project, and what makes an EB-5 success story. This chapter delves more into practicalities and focuses on where the EB-5 funds fit within a particular project's overall financing. Once you have decided that EB-5 investments are an appropriate fit for your project and goals, it is time to determine how you will structure your capital stack.

DEFINING CAPITAL STACK

The "capital stack" refers to the totality of capital invested in a project. Total development costs are financed through a combination of pure debt, hybrid debt (containing an equity component), and pure equity. Within each of these three broad categories are sub-classifications and priorities, including security interests on various assets, priorities on each such security interest and priorities for payment (usually called the "waterfall"). In project finance, the safest capital—the capital with first payment priority and the most senior liens on the most important collateral—is considered the base of the capital stack. The riskiest capital is considered the top of the capital stack. Investors at the higher tiers of the capital stack generally expect to be compensated for taking on a greater risk. This compensation is usually in the form of a higher return if the project is successful and pays off the lower tiers of the capital stack.

THE CAPITAL STACK AND MARKETABILITY

The capital stack has an impact on the project's marketability. The willingness of the developer to deploy and keep its own capital at risk in the highest (i.e., the riskiest) tier of the capital stack is probably the single most important criteria for underwriting a project. Remember, the most knowledgeable investor in a project is the developer of the project; showing that you trust your business plans enough to put your money at stake will appeal to investors who are putting their money at risk. The EB-5 investor, like other investors, wants the sponsor to have significant skin in the game.

In the first few years following the EB-5 program's 2008 resurgence, it was possible for projects to find investors to fund 100 percent of the development capital. Those days are gone. Today, it is extremely difficult to market a project in China without substantial developer equity that remains at risk. As the developer, if you don't place your own capital in a tier that carries greater risk, investors will assume you do not have full confidence that your project will succeed.

Today, if EB-5 capital is in first lien position—that is, at the bottom of the capital stack—most migration agents in China prefer that EB-5 capital make up no more than 70 percent of the capital invested in the project. Generally, the developer's contribution of unimproved land is either not considered capital invested or is considered capital invested only as to the hard costs of the land (contrasted with today's claimed fair market value of the land). This market standard permits only slightly more leverage than what traditional senior lenders require for a first lien construction loan.

THE CAPITAL STACK'S MEZZANINE TIER

If the project has a traditional senior lender at the base of the capital stack, the EB-5 capital will be in the form of equity or subordinated debt. The EB-5 capital may have a subordinate security interest on all or a subset of the assets or the sponsor's equity in the project, or it may be unsecured. Though subordinate to senior lenders, the EB-5 capital will normally be senior to the developer equity. It will therefore occupy a middle tier of the capital stack. In project finance, a hybrid or pure debt slice in the middle of the capital stack is often called "mezzanine" finance. For mezzanine level finance, Chinese migration agents will often insist on minimum developer equity of between 10 and 20 percent, depending on other project qualities.

Tip

Though counterintuitive, many migration agents prefer mezzanine level deals to first lien deals because of the implicit validation from the due diligence presumably performed by the senior lender. This is the case notwithstanding that the senior lender has generally underwritten only the project's ability to pay its preferred position in the waterfall.

In general, the Chinese migration agents (and investors) look favorably upon government support of the capital stack in the form of tax credits or loan guarantees for senior debt. (The more government support, the more appealing the project.)

CAPITAL STACK AND JOB CREATION

For job count purposes (crucial for investors to get their green cards), the number of jobs created by a project is determined based on the project as a whole. This is an important concept to understand. The larger the percentage of the capital stack made up by EB-5 investment (therefore, the greater the number of individual investors), the fewer of the total number of jobs created are allocated to each EB-5 investor. In the EB-5 industry, the number or percentage of jobs in excess of the required 10 per investor is referred to as the "job buffer." The job buffer increases the likelihood of all investors receiving their visas, even if USCIS disagrees with some aspects of the job-creation calculation or some projected jobs are not created as a result of things not going as planned.

Chinese migration agents usually demand a job buffer of at least 20 percent of the jobs projected in the economist's report. That is, the number of jobs needed at the rate of 10 per investor normally cannot exceed 80 percent of the jobs projected in the economist's report if the project is to be marketed successfully through these agents. Higher job buffers are always a positive factor in marketability. Where riskier economic methodologies are used (or where jobs are counted in areas USCIS frequently challenges, such as guest expenditures, tenant occupancy or direct construction), Chinese migration agents may demand even higher job buffers as a condition for accepting the mandate to market the project.

Example: If a TEA-located project's total construction cost is $8.5 million and its business plan claims 170 jobs will be created based on the economist's report, the project can theoretically support 17 EB-5 investors (each with a $500,000 investment), permitting the entire construction cost to be funded with EB-5 capital. If EB-5 investors put in the full $8.5 million, there will be no job buffer. If USCIS successfully challenges even one job, at least one investor will not receive a visa. On the other hand, if the project raises only $3 million in EB-5 capital, then the 170 jobs are allocated to only six investors, resulting in over 28 jobs per investor. This would be a much more attractive project for investors because of the higher likelihood of visa approval.

STRUCTURING THE EB-5 INVESTMENT

The seminal case that sets the precedent for EB-5 investment requirements is *Matter of Izummi. Izummi* stated that the term "invest" does not include a contribution of capital in exchange for a note, bond, convertible debt, obligation, or any other debt arrangement between the immigrant investor and the new commercial enterprise.

The Loan Model

So how is it that EB-5 investments are often structured as debt? The answer is separating the business into "two enterprises"—the new commercial enterprise and the job-creating enterprise. This allows one enterprise to loan investment capital to the other enterprise. The new commercial enterprise sells equity to EB-5 investors and then uses those funds to make a loan to the job-creating enterprise (i.e., the "project"), which in turn spends the capital and creates the jobs. This structure results in a true equity investment by the EB-5 investors, though the underlying investment is an undivided interest in a loan receivable from the project. This structure is available only for investments under regional center sponsorship.

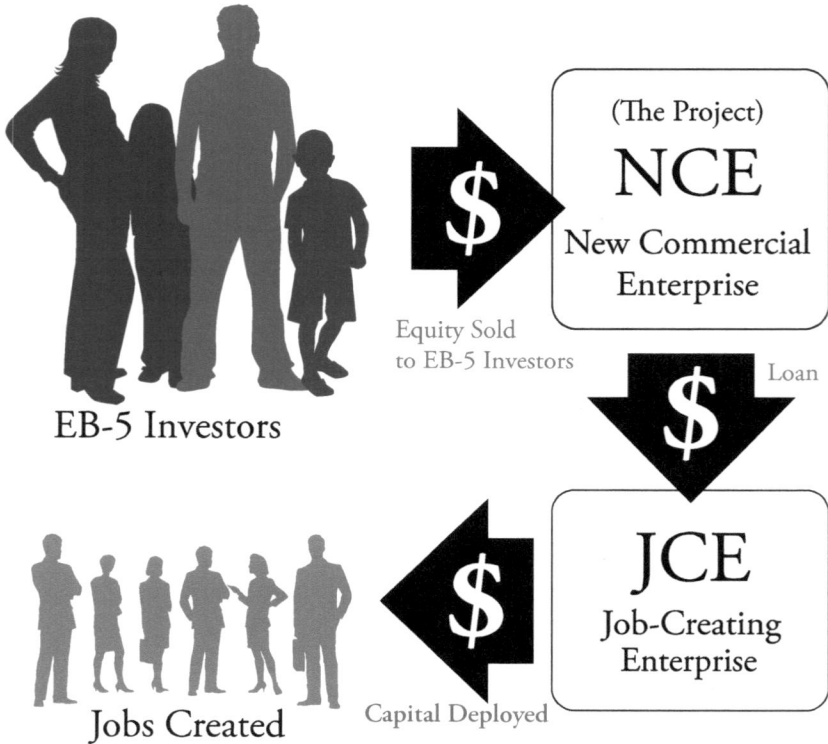

The loan to the job-creating enterprise may be secured or unsecured and may have whatever waterfall characteristics desired, as long as they are agreeable to the developer and the investors (or the Chinese marketing agents, as the investors' proxies). Currently, interest rates on these loans range from 5 percent to 8 percent, where interest is received by the new commercial enterprise and then used to pay the promised return to EB-5 investors, operating costs of the new commercial enterprise, and/or profits to the regional center or other promoter(s) of the EB-5 capital raise. The promised return to EB-5 investors is usually 0.5 to 2 percent, with 1 percent being the most common. EB-5 investors normally consider the amount of promised return to be a distant third on their list of concerns—behind receiving a green card and having their capital returned. A typical loan term is five years. Five years allows sufficient time for the investors to receive a conditional visa and to subsequently have the conditions removed, resulting in a permanent green card. This also keeps the investment "at risk" throughout the visa process, which is a requirement of the EB-5 program. Some deals permit a limited number of one- or two- year extensions on the loan maturity date, sometimes with an increased interest rate paid during each extension.

When the loan is repaid, the new commercial enterprise has no further purpose for existence. It therefore liquidates, returning the original investment and any unpaid amount of the promised investment return to the investors. Any other funds remaining in the new commercial enterprise are then distributed to an affiliate of the developer or the regional center in its role as general partner or manager of the new commercial enterprise.

The Equity Model

Equity models are an alternative to the loan model. Occasionally, but rarely in larger syndicated projects, EB-5 investors may receive true equity in the job-creating enterprise—the highest tier of risk in the capital stack. In most cases, true equity appeals neither to the investors nor the developer. Investors usually want priority over the developer equity, and the developer usually does not want to share its full upside with EB-5 investors, who normally do not ascribe value to that kind of return on an EB-5 investment.

The Preferred Equity Model. A more common equity model is preferred equity. Preferred equity has a preference over the developer equity for the promised return on investment and for the return of the investment. The return is often capped at the promised return, which is again in the 0.5 to 2 percent range, with 1 percent being the most common. Preferred equity may be issued from the project (the job-creating enterprise) directly to EB-5 investors or may be issued from the job-creating enterprise to a separate new commercial enterprise, which more closely mimics the loan model. There are advantages and disadvantages to each structure that should be discussed with sophisticated corporate and securities attorneys.

The main driver for preferred equity over the loan model is the requirements of the senior lender. Many senior lenders will prohibit subordinate debt, or offer less favorable terms if subordinate debt is allowed. Some lenders may further prohibit any equity in the project from having a "put" right or redemption feature, which could otherwise roughly mimic a loan maturity date. It is important to note here that current EB-5 adjudication policy prevents EB-5 investors, prior to the end of the two-year conditional residence period, from having a put or redemption right for their direct equity in the new commercial enterprise, even if such right does not become available until after the conditions of the visa are removed. However, the EB-5 program rules do allow the new commercial enterprise itself to have a put or redemption right against the job-creating enterprise, and once such a right has been successfully exercised and the new commercial enterprise has been paid in full for its investment in the job creating enterprise, the new commercial enterprise will generally liquidate and return capital to EB-5 investors. Where the senior lender prohibits a put or redemption right in favor of the new commercial enterprise, the preferred equity should have other features that incentivize the job-creating enterprise to pay off the EB-5 capital so investors can receive a return of capital at the end of the expected hold period.

While the EB-5 marketplace has come to understand and accept the models in this chapter, every project is different, and it is critical to obtain the advice of sophisticated corporate and securities attorneys that:

- understand all of the legal ramifications of different capital designs; and

- have the skill, experience, and budget to modify the standard designs as needed to meet all of EB-5 program requirements, market realities, and the needs of the developers and the other capital stack investors.

COMPLYING WITH THE "AT RISK" EB-5 REQUIREMENT

The EB-5 visa program requires that EB-5 investment capital be "at risk," and that requirement was further defined in the Izummi case and in the USCIS Policy Memorandum from May 30, 2013. Developers and regional center operators therefore have become familiar with the nuances of the "at risk" requirement and in turn need to structure their deals in a way that complies with this requirement.

First, EB-5 capital may not be used to pay expenses of raising the EB-5 capital. Broker fees, migration agent fees, attorney fees, economist fees, marketing fees, and other costs of the capital raise must be paid from another capital source or from project revenues once it is operational. Most EB-5 offerings require investors to pay an administrative fee of around $50,000, in addition to the at risk capital. The full investment amount in a TEA-located project is therefore generally $550,000, with $500,000 deployed exclusively to the job-creating activity and the balance used to offset costs. The administrative fee is usually not refundable to investors except in limited circumstances involving visa denial at the I-526 stage. The administrative fee is also usually "non-accountable," meaning that projects rarely are required to provide any after-the-fact accounting to investors of how they used the administrative fee.

Second, an EB-5 investor cannot enter into a redemption agreement at any time prior to the end of the two-year conditional residence. The investor must enter into the investment not knowing:

1. whether he or she will be able to sell the interest after receipt of permanent residency; and

2. what price he or she would actually obtain for such interest.

Accordingly, an investor cannot have a traditional put right—the right to force the new commercial enterprise to buy back his or her interest at a price determined in advance, such as the original investment amount.

Third, reserve funds that are not made available for the purposes of job creation are not considered at risk. Funds may be used for contingency expenses, but such funds must be available for use in the business's day-to-day operations. In *Izummi*, funds were set aside to buy back the investors' partnership interests in the future. USCIS considered this set aside to violate the at risk requirement.

Some common features of EB-5 offerings do not violate the at risk requirement under current USCIS adjudication policy. If the investment is placed into an escrow account that irrevocably commits the release of the capital contingent only upon I-526 approval, the capital is still considered at risk. If the investor receives a return on his investment that is (a) not guaranteed and (b) not a portion of his or her capital, the initial capital investment is considered "at risk." Thus, a project can distribute out of profits a return to the investor, as is usually done in the loan and equity structures summarized above.

BRIDGE CAPITAL

Bridge financing is an important project finance tool both inside and outside the EB-5 market. Bridge financing is particularly important for EB-5 capital because of the long time frames between commencing work for an EB-5 offering and the availability of capital for expenditure on the project.

USCIS has historically been wary of bridge capital in EB-5 projects, often asking in Requests for Evidence (RFEs) whether the project would not have created the jobs, "but for" the EB-5 capital. The EB-5 community refers to this as the "but for" requirement. The USCIS May 30, 2013 Policy Memorandum substantially eased the but-for requirement, indicating that if the project commences based on bridge financing prior to the receipt of the EB-5 capital and subsequently replaces it with EB-5 capital, the new commercial enterprise may still receive credit for the job creation.

Tip

According to the May 30, 2013 USCIS Policy Memorandum, the replacement of bridge financing with EB-5 investor capital should generally have been contemplated prior to acquiring the original non-EB-5 financing. However, even if the EB-5 financing was not contemplated prior to acquiring the temporary financing, as long as the financing to be replaced was contemplated as short-term temporary financing that would be subsequently replaced, the infusion of EB-5 financing could still result in the creation of and credit for new jobs.

Despite its importance, bridge financing has been a challenge for EB-5 deals:

1. because of legal uncertainty as to the but-for requirement (largely resolved by the USCIS May 30, 2013 Policy Memorandum but still on the minds of many investors); and

2. because of a lack of understanding about EB-5 amongst traditional bridge lenders.

Presently, a number of banks and specialty lenders have developed bridge capital products for the time that EB-5 funds remain in escrow pending visa milestones. These lenders generally accept the risk of visa denials (which would cause escrowed funds not to be released), but not the risk either of the failure to raise EB-5 funds or of an economic failure of the project.

Another common source of bridge capital is the developer's own equity. If the developer finances a part of the capital stack with its own equity, the developer can pay development costs as incurred and then take out some of its equity with EB-5 capital. The EB-5 capital is usually much cheaper than the opportunity cost of the developer's own capital, and the takeout enables the developer to use its capital for its next project. The use of EB-5 proceeds to take out developer equity must be disclosed in the offering materials, and if too little developer equity will remain after the takeout, the offering may not be marketable.

CONCLUSION

An effective capital stack requires careful design and close collaboration among the developers, the regional center, the EB-5 professionals, and the other sources of capital. An effective capital stack often requires ingenuity consistent with fundamentals in much the same way that a space-optimizing architectural design must be consistent with the laws of physics.

The total cost of capital must be sufficiently less than the expected profits of the enterprise to rationalize the project economically. Capital must be available when needed for the development schedule. Each tier of the capital stack must fit harmoniously with the other tiers, and agreements (like inter-creditor agreements) may be necessary to anticipate and address potential conflicts among different tiers of the capital stack. A successful EB-5 project requires careful planning of the capital stack. Capital stack engineering is not an exercise in "templates." The quality and experience of the professionals that assist will have a direct effect on the short- and long-term success of the EB-5 capital raise.

CHAPTER 8: WHAT ARE MY REGIONAL CENTER OPTIONS?

By Jeff Campion and David Hirson

Up until now, you have been evaluating whether EB-5 is right for your project. You have weighed the differences between EB-5 capital and traditional capital, you have familiarized yourself with the characteristics that make an EB-5 project successful and marketable, and you have contemplated how to use EB-5 in the capital stack. Now, it is time to move forward and actually get into the EB-5 game. To do this, you need to decide whether your raise will be "direct" or employ a regional center. This chapter will explain the differences between the options and how you can raise capital using the EB-5 program.

THE DIRECT INVESTMENT

Although an overwhelming majority of EB-5 investments are not direct, direct investments have certain advantages. It is important to at least understand the direct approach so you can compare it with the regional center approach before deciding which will work better for your project and the EB-5 investors who might invest in it. The direct investment method is usually chosen by one of two parties: a foreign entrepreneur looking to establish a new business in the United States or a developer looking for smaller EB-5 capital raise amounts. Common direct EB-5 projects include restaurants, franchises, retail stores, and tech start-ups. From the sponsors' perspective, one benefit of going direct is that you do not need regional center designation from USCIS. This avoids the time and/or cost of obtaining USCIS designation for your own regional center or affiliating with someone else's regional center.

Capital Requirements

Whether an EB-5 investment is direct or made through a regional center-affiliated project, the minimum capital requirement is still the same: $500,000 if located within a targeted employment area (TEA) or $1 million if not located in a TEA. As mentioned in the introduction to Part II, a TEA is defined as either a rural area or a high unemployment area.

Job Creation

As explained in more detail below, the most important difference between direct EB-5 investments and regional center EB-5 investments is job creation. All EB-5 cases (except investments in a "troubled business") require the new commercial enterprise to create at least 10 full-time jobs for U.S. workers per EB-5 investor. The difference, however, is that investors in direct EB-5 cases can count only jobs of specific, identifiable people who work full-time directly as employees of the new commercial enterprise. In contrast, investors in regional center cases can rely on "reasonable methodologies," such as economic input-output models, to also show the creation of "indirect" and "induced" jobs. Indirect jobs are those created outside of the new commercial enterprise by the EB-5 investor's investment. The ability to count indirect and induced jobs is a major advantage of regional center investments over direct investments and is one of the major reasons that the vast majority of investors make indirect investments through regional centers instead of direct investments. If you are only looking to raise a limited amount of EB-5 capital, and your project will have a requisite number of identifiable people who work full-time as employees, the direct investment method may be the right choice for you.

THE REGIONAL CENTER INVESTMENT

With the regional center method, the foreign investor invests in an enterprise under a USCIS-designated EB-5 regional center. This investment method is best for larger-scale syndicated investments, though it could certainly also be used (and sometimes is used) for very small projects, some as small as a few investors.

Capital Requirements

As mentioned above, all EB-5 investments face the same legal minimum investment requirement, which is either $500,000 for projects in TEAs or $1 million for projects outside of TEAs. Most—but not all—regional center projects are located in TEAs.

Job Creation, Including "Indirect" and "Induced" Jobs

As mentioned above, EB-5 investors who invest through regional centers can count all jobs that flow from the investment: direct jobs, indirect jobs, and induced jobs. USCIS defines "direct" jobs to be those of employees who work directly for the new commercial enterprise. Economists generally use a somewhat different definition of "direct" employment, but in either case, direct jobs are the primary employment arising from the creation and operation of the project, such as a hotel.

"Indirect" and "induced" jobs flow secondarily from the EB-5 investor's investment. Indirect jobs are those created by other companies that produce the goods or provide the services needed for the construction and operation of the regional center-based project. This includes the companies that provide concrete, steel, engineering services, etc. for the construction and that provide the furniture, equipment, supplies, accounting services, etc. for the operations. Induced jobs are those created when the employees of the construction company, the operations company, and the supplier

> Under the direct EB-5 approach, a $100 million EB-5 capital raise for a large hotel would require 200 investors (at $500,000 per investor) and 10 jobs for each of those investors, for a total job-creation requirement of 2,000 jobs. Even five-star hotels likely fall well short of employing 2,000 people in a $100 million project. Using the economic forecasting models allowed in a regional center investment, an economist could segregate and input the total costs across each industry sector of the project to generate an overall job-creation number. Because the models work on multipliers, job counts for such a $100 million hotel project would safely support a very large number of EB-5 investors. Essentially, if USCIS finds the economic models sound, the project will typically need to prove only that it spent the money as inputted into the model and constructed the project as detailed in the business plan. Expenditure and project construction will typically be enough in the eyes of USCIS to determine that the jobs have been created. (Unlike direct EB-5 cases, regional center cases do not require proof of each specific job created, a task that can be unpredictable and time-consuming.)

companies go out into the community and spend their earnings to buy goods and services, such as housing, groceries, cable television, legal services, etc., in turn creating even more jobs for the providers of those goods and services. Economists use economic models to account for indirect and induced jobs created by EB-5 projects.

From the investor's perspective, the regional center program's allowance for counting "indirect" and "induced" jobs is a great benefit, but from a planning perspective, it is important to consider that such regional center projects also provide the investor with virtually no control. If an individual wants to start his or her own business or expand a preexisting one (and therefore truly manage the investment and company operations) a direct investment without syndication to other investors method may be the better option. Ultimately, choosing between direct investment and regional center investment is a great topic for an investor to discuss with his or her investment adviser or qualified legal counsel.

BECOME A REGIONAL CENTER OR AFFILIATE WITH ONE

If an investor or developer is at a point where the dollars required for project completion far outweigh the number of "direct" jobs the project can create, a regional center program may be the only option. Direct investment simply does not produce enough jobs in most EB-5 deals. Once you decide that a regional center approach is better for your project, you have to decide whether to start an EB-5 regional center yourself or affiliate with an existing one. As with other questions in EB-5, the answer depends on your particular situation.

Establishing an EB-5 regional center is a lengthy process and comes at a substantial cost. Regional center applications are required to be accompanied by incorporation documents, business plans, economic impact reports, feasibility reports, and so on. Production of these documents requires a lot of planning time, a unified approach, and the assistance of experienced professionals.

Affiliating with a regional center allows projects to move forward immediately. Developers can enter into shared services agreements with an already-designated regional center, essentially allowing the project to use the regional center's USCIS designation to sponsor the project and gain the benefit of counting direct, indirect, and induced jobs. The project can begin soliciting investors immediately and investors can file the subsequent applications without further delay. The downside of affiliating may be cost and control. Affiliating with a regional center may come with an equal or even greater cost than starting your own regional center. The fees for affiliating often vary with project size and there is an extremely wide range of fees prevailing based on supply and demand of regional centers in the particular geography and industry. Moreover, you are depending on a third party to maintain its designation to operate as an EB-5 regional center, which means you lose control of this aspect of the process. If the regional center loses its designation for reasons independent from your project, your project will be negatively affected.

HOW TO BECOME A REGIONAL CENTER

As we mentioned briefly in the introduction, an EB-5 regional center is any economic unit, public or private, involved in the promotion of economic growth. Governmental agencies, partnerships, corporations, and additional existing U.S. commercial entities can qualify for regional center designation. USCIS designation entails a multi-step process that requires the input of various experts. The cost of obtaining regional center designation is highly variable. The Form I-924 (Application for Regional Center Under the Immigrant Investor Pilot Program) currently costs $6,230 to file with USCIS. However, the overall preparation and filing cost is often far more, and largely dependent on the fees charged by various EB-5 experts. The total cost could easily exceed $100,000, depending on circumstances. However, if you are planning a large capital raise, or multiple capital raises, this start-up cost could save many multiples of the total cost over time or even for the first project.

Types of Regional Center Filings

The EB-5 Handbook is designed to give you the general scope of the EB-5 program as well as some specifics that you will most likely discuss with your EB-5 professional team before filing. If you decide to file an I-924 regional center application, your EB-5 professional team will help you determine which one of the three categories to use when presenting your project within the application: hypothetical, actual, and exemplar ("shovel ready").

In addition, the choice of presenting a hypothetical project, an actual project, or an exemplar project typically will affect how much, if any, deference USCIS will commit to your project within the language of the letter approving your application for regional center designation. Any deference that USCIS spells out in its designation letter will be applied to the project-related documentation that your EB-5 investors subsequently submit to USCIS with their I-526 petitions.

In general, the most appropriate approach will depend on how well formulated your project is and how close you are to beginning construction. Below are more details about what exactly is required for each type of project scenario in your application and how much, if any, deference USCIS will attach to that project approval.

Hypothetical. Of the three possible options, the "hypothetical" project is the least developed presentation of your proposed project. In many cases, it will be only a general description of the type of project you might someday complete in the future. USCIS's May 30, 2013 memorandum on EB-5 describes it this way: "A 'hypothetical project' refers to a project proposal that is not supported by a Matter of Ho compliant business plan." (As discussed in more detail below, "Matter of

Ho compliant business plan" means, practically speaking, a relatively complete and detailed business plan.) A back-of-envelope plan or a simple one or two page summary of what the project is going to be may not be enough for a hypothetical project, but USCIS likely will not require a full-blown business plan of a hypothetical project. In turn, because a "hypothetical" project is by its own terms not detailed, if you later develop such a project based on your initial hypothetical analysis, USCIS will give the investors' I-526 petitions no "deference" at all. USCIS will analyze the actual project documentation at the time that investors submit it with their I-526 petitions. Proposing a hypothetical project is less time-consuming in the beginning, but offers no help for later adjudication of I-526 petitions. Nonetheless, many EB-5 projects that have started with a hypothetical project in an I-924 have successfully produced visas for the real project.

Actual. "Actual" projects are the middle ground between "hypothetical" projects and "exemplar" projects. If you submit an "actual" project, USCIS will want to see a detailed project description, construction timelines, detailed budgets, analysis of market and competitors, and so on (i.e., "a Matter of Ho compliant business plan"). In submitting an "actual" project instead of a "hypothetical" one, you are essentially asking USCIS to approve both the regional center application and the actual project itself. In return for such specific and detailed documentation to review, if USCIS approves the regional center application with an "actual" project, USCIS will "accord deference to subsequent filings under the project involving the same material facts and issues."

Exemplar. "Exemplar" projects are actual projects that are "shovel ready." "Exemplar" projects require the regional center applicant to provide the most detailed information, but in return, if USCIS approves the regional center application with the "exemplar" project, USCIS will be providing the highest level of deference to future I-526 petitions filed with respect to this exemplar project. An approved exemplar project will have been determined to meet all project-based requirements for an investor's EB-5 application.

An important point to keep in mind with respect to any USCIS deference: irrespective of whether USCIS has approved a regional center application with a "hypothetical" project, an "actual" project, or an "exemplar" project, USCIS always reserves the right to deny an I-526 petition based on issues related to whether the specific investor's source of investment funds are lawful.

Filing a Regional Center Application (I-924)

Perhaps the most important step of the regional center application process is hiring the right team. The following sections are categorized into sections as to whom or what you may encounter along the way.

The Business Plan. The business plan is one of the most important documents required for regional center filing. Hiring a good business plan writer with expertise in producing EB-5-compliant business plans can be a big help in presenting a strong application. Such business plan writers should follow the Matter of Ho precedent decision, which describes the standards by which USCIS will review a business plan:

> *The plan should contain a market analysis, including the names of competing businesses and their relative strengths and weaknesses, a comparison of the competition's products and pricing structures, and a description of the target market/prospective customers of the new commercial enterprise. The plan should list the required permits and licenses obtained. If applicable, it should describe the manufacturing or production process, the materials required, and the supply sources. The plan should detail any contracts executed for the supply of materials and/or the distribution of products. It should discuss the marketing strategy of the business, including pricing, advertising, and servicing. The plan should set forth the business's organizational structure and its personnel's experience. It should explain the business's staffing requirements and contain a timetable for hiring, as well as job descriptions for all positions. It should contain sales, cost, and income projections and detail the bases therefore. Most importantly, the business plan must be credible.[1]*

The Economic Report. Your team will also include an economist, hired to prepare job calculation and job-creation reports. For the purpose of demonstrating indirect job creation, petitioners must employ reasonable economic methodologies to establish, by a preponderance of the evidence, that the required infusion of capital or creation of direct jobs will result in a certain number of indirect jobs. The economist can also help your team determine whether the regional center's proposed project is located in a TEA. If the project is located in a TEA, then the required EB-5 investment amount for each immigrant investor is lowered from $1 million to $500,000.

Securities/Corporate Attorney. Your team will most likely include a securities/corporate attorney who has relevant experience in producing EB-5-compliant subscription agreements, private placement memorandums (PPM), and sometimes related documentation, such as limited partnership agreements, loan agreements, affiliation agreements, etc. These documents must not only

---

1. Administrative Appeals Office. *Interim Decision #3362.*

comply with SEC federal regulations, but also with USCIS regulations, such as the "at risk" requirement mentioned above. In particular, securities/corporate attorneys will be keeping an eye out for any clause providing a put, call, or redemption of investment funds, because such provisions may violate the "at risk" provision and may result in denial of the investors' EB-5 petitions (either the I-526 petition or the I-829 petition).

Immigration Attorney. The vast majority of successful EB-5 regional center development teams include an immigration lawyer with significant EB-5 experience. Immigration attorneys will typically coordinate and review all work proposed by other professionals involved in the regional center application effort and will shepherd the regional center application process. In addition, immigration lawyers with significant prior EB-5 experience will be able to advise regional centers, projects, and EB-5 investors through each step of the overall compliance process.

USCIS Processing. Once the EB-5 regional center team completes all of the necessary documentation—the business plan, economic report, offering documents, etc.—the immigration lawyer will file the I-924 application with USCIS. Processing times vary—sometimes greatly—but current average processing times are around a year. In the meantime, USCIS does not object to marketing the project before your I-924 petition is approved. However, your investors will not be able to file their I-526 petitions until USCIS approves the regional center application and it can be very difficult to market a project that is awaiting regional center designation because of the uncertainty involved. In terms of planning, you will need to take this timing into account when trying to estimate exactly when the investors' funds will be available for the project.

HOW TO AFFILIATE WITH A REGIONAL CENTER

Due to the time and expense required, becoming an EB-5 regional center may not be the best option for your particular situation. This next section discusses how a project affiliates with an EB-5 regional center as opposed to getting USCIS designation, including:

- the process of finding the right regional center
- key questions to ask of regional centers
- affiliating with the regional center and structuring an EB-5 deal
- the documents normally executed when affiliating

- whether purchasing a regional center is an option

Finding the Right Regional Center

There are a variety of methods used to contact the principals of regional centers. One way is through the developer's general counsel or through an immigration attorney who works in the EB-5 space. The reality is that, while there are around 500 or so EB-5 regional centers that have been designated by USCIS, the number of regional centers that are active and know the EB-5 space well is small. With that being said, an immigration attorney who works in the field may know which regional centers work within your project's geographical region. Alternatively, USCIS regularly updates a list of approved EB-5 regional centers on its website. You can use the information they provide to research online and call them individually.

Key Questions to Ask of EB-5 Regional Centers

Once you have located a few regional centers that may be candidates for affiliation, you need to ask several key questions. Your immigration lawyer can assist you with asking the right questions and ensuring that the answers you receive are complete, accurate, and acceptable before you decide to go forward with an affiliation arrangement with an existing regional center. In particular, you and your immigration lawyer will want to review the regional center's USCIS designation letter very carefully, which details the geographic area; the approved industries; the economic methodology used; and which documents, if any, USCIS is also approving along with the regional center designation itself (e.g., the offering documents, the business plan, and other documentation). When reviewing the USCIS designation letter and related documents, you and your immigration lawyer will need to find out the following information about the regional center you are inquiring to affiliate with:

1. *What is the geographical boundary of the regional center?* It is important to know whether your project is located within the geographical boundaries of the regional center. If not, an amendment is technically not required, but if your immigration lawyer feels that an amendment should still be filed, you need to remember that this process will take time for USCIS approval.

2. *Are there any approvals, denials, or requests for evidence (RFEs) issued by USCIS with respect to the regional center?* It is important to understand the current affairs of the regional center, whether there are any possible issues with its license, how the regional center has responded to the issues in the past, and how it will respond to issues in the future. The regional center will

be a developer's partner for a long time, so it will be critical to understand how the regional center will interact with the developer.

3. *Do the regional center principals have sufficient experience in the EB-5 space, either on their own or through their professionals?* It is generally preferable to affiliate with a regional center whose principals have EB-5 experience, but this may not be possible. If not, it is important to look at the EB-5 professionals who are part of the regional center team.

4. *Has the regional center filed its I-924A forms, the supplemental form to the I-924?* This form is a simple yearly reporting requirement, but if it is not filed, USCIS could decide to revoke the regional center designation. Therefore, it is important to confirm that the form has been filed on a yearly basis.

Affiliating with a Regional Center and Structuring an EB-5 Deal

Assuming that your initial due diligence is complete and you are comfortable with your regional center selection, the next issue is structuring the deal with the regional center. When affiliating with a regional center, the relationship can take on at least three forms: a simple administration agreement, an agreement by the regional center to loan the money to the project (sometimes referred to as the "job-creating enterprise"), or a hybrid.

Recap of Entities Involved. Before looking at the types of affiliation relationships, it is important to review the difference among the regional center entity, the new commercial enterprise (NCE), and the "job-creating enterprise" (JCE). The regional center itself is simply the entity that USCIS has designated as having the authority to sponsor investments from overseas investors who want to file for green cards through the EB-5 program. Although theoretically it could, the regional center entity itself virtually never accepts EB-5 investor funds; instead, it may manage the new commercial enterprise that accepts investor funds or it may perform only the limited functions of a regional center related to EB-5 program requirements. In an equity model, the new commercial enterprise may carry out the project itself. In a loan model and in some equity models, the new commercial enterprise loans or invests the money into the job-creating enterprise, which carries out the project.

Recap of Tasks to Be Completed. Before you can agree to "affiliate," it is critical to understand exactly who does what. This includes developing the project, raising the capital, preparing documentation for the investors and USCIS, and so on. Be sure to discuss these issues with your immigration attorney to ensure that you know exactly what you are paying and what you are receiving in return. You will be seriously disappointed if you assume that the other party is going to take care of something and then it turns out that the agreements clearly state that task (such as raising money) is your responsibility.

The Administration Agreement. At the lowest level of affiliation between the regional center and the developer that "affiliates" with the regional center, the regional center and the developer may agree to simply allow the project to affiliate with the regional center through an administration agreement. In this instance, the regional center is simply fulfilling its reporting requirements to USCIS based on the information provided to it from the project and ensuring that the project is progressing as it is supposed to. Without the regional center playing a control role in this scenario, the developer has the most flexibility but also the most responsibility for getting the work done. In addition, the developer could set up and control both the new commercial enterprise and the job-creating enterprise. Such an approach has both advantages and disadvantages that you will want to discuss carefully with your lawyers and others on your EB-5 professional team.

Regional Center Loan Model. On the other extreme, the regional center (or an affiliate) would form the new commercial enterprise and be the manager or general partner of the new commercial enterprise. In turn, the new commercial enterprise would loan the money to the job-creating enterprise. In this instance, the developer is just a commercial borrower from the regional center (or affiliate) acting as a commercial lender. The regional center (or affiliate) has substantially all of the responsibilities associated with raising the EB-5 funds and managing the life cycle of the EB-5 program.

A Hybrid. Between the two extremes, there are hybrid scenarios, in which some of the other duties are shared between the regional center and the developer. For example, the regional center might do more than just fulfill its reporting requirements to USCIS by additionally providing introductions to broker-dealers or investment advisers in the United States or migration agents in China or other countries—or perhaps even flying to countries with the developer to make personal introductions. In this scenario, the regional center would have no direct control role in the new commercial entity itself, but would instead be performing more services than simply the administrative ones.

Of course, the cost of the affiliation arrangement is likely to vary by the level of services provided. A simple administration agreement would be expected to be the least expensive for the developer in terms of what is paid to the regional center, while the regional center affiliate loaning the money to the project (the loan model) would likely be the most expensive—assuming the regional center is taking on the role of raising the money, too.

It is critical not to be shortsighted and assume that the least expensive option is the best. If you choose a simple administrative relationship, you will likely be spending substantial time and resources to raise the money and deal with investors on an ongoing basis. Many times, the most time- and cost- efficient manner for a developer to proceed is to simply borrow from a third party that handles the regional center and raises the EB-5 capital. Once the relationship is defined, the documents reflecting such must be prepared. In all cases, however, the approach you select can have a major impact on the overall profitability and success of your development project, so it is critical to think these options through carefully and discuss them thoroughly with your immigration lawyer.

Documents for Affiliating with a Regional Center

There are essential documents that must be executed to affiliate with the regional center. Moreover, depending on the relationship, there may be more documents to which the regional center (or an affiliated entity) is party. The essential documents may have different names, but they contain the same key ingredients:

- an agreement between the regional center and the new commercial enterprise;
- a fee agreement (memorandum of understanding); and
- in a regional center loan model, documents ensuring that the job-creating enterprise complies with the terms of the loan

There needs to be an agreement between the regional center and the new commercial enterprise (into which EB-5 capital will be invested). This is normally an administrative services agreement, sometimes known as a memorandum of understanding, that spells out the relationship between the new commercial enterprise and the regional center, and that the project is part of the regional center. Second, there is a fee agreement that is normally executed among the new commercial enterprise, the job-creating enterprise, and regional center for the services to be provided. Third, in a regional center loan model, there will be a loan agreement, security agreements, and other related documents ensuring that the job-creating entity complies with the terms of the loan. These are all issues to discuss with your attorney and others on your team of EB-5 professionals.

PURCHASING A REGIONAL CENTER

Instead of becoming a regional center or affiliating with one, the developer could choose to purchase a regional center or become a partner in a regional center with the current owners.

Although not common, sales of regional centers have transpired. The rapidly increasing number of regional center designations and the increasing competition to find investors may result in sales of regional centers becoming more common, as the realities of the industry force weak operations to sell rather than continue to pay the cost of maintaining a dormant regional center.

Though likely to increase in the future, selling a regional center is still a rarity, and the rules related to sales are not that clear. There have, however, been successful cases in the past. If you want to go down this path, you need to keep in mind that the ownership-transfer process may take about the same time as filing an I-924 application for a new regional center designation. Bearing this in mind, it may make better sense to file for a new regional center or to affiliate with an existing one. You should also be aware that the language of I-924 approvals leaves room for debate, with such wording as, "the regional center designation is non-transferrable, as any changes in management of the regional center will require the approval of an amendment to the approved regional center designation." While the designation cannot be transferred from one entity to another, it is unclear as to what the "non-transferability" of the designation has to do with a change in management or a change in ownership of the initial entity designated. Arguably, no designation is being transferred, but USCIS has not clarified this issue yet, though it may do so in the future.

CONCLUSION

Choosing how you will raise EB-5 capital—whether directly or through a regional center—is a decision that must be weighed carefully. Even after you have made that basic choice, there are even further considerations to be made under the regional center rubric—to file or affiliate. This chapter should have given you some insight into which option is best for your particular situation. If you decide that filing for your own regional center is too time consuming and costly, with the proper team of professionals, a developer can successfully affiliate with a regional center and have a mutually beneficial relationship. This is a major decision with substantial impact on your overall likelihood of success and profitability. If you are considering this approach you should discuss it early on with your attorney and EB-5 professional team, so you can determine the best path forward for your particular project and vision.

CHAPTER 9: HOW DO I RAISE EB-5 CAPITAL?

By Jeff Campion, Linda He, Linda Lau, Joseph McCarthy, Reid Thomas, and John Tishler

By now you understand the EB-5 program, whether it is right for your project, how to structure your capital stack, and how to prepare to accept investments. After all those anxious months waiting for your EB-5 regional center approval or working out affiliation agreements, you're finally ready to roll. At this point, most regional centers are left with a single daunting question: Now what? Chapter 9 will walk you through the steps of actually raising the EB-5 capital that will fund your project.

Before you are ready to fly around the world to market your project, or accept any investment, you must go through the proper preparations. First you will want to decide whether and how you are going to escrow the capital that is invested in your project as investors are waiting for their immigration decisions. These escrow arrangements are important not only for marketing the project to investors who want to be sure that their capital is safe, but they are also important for you as you plan the timing of your project. After you have determined the appropriate escrow arrangement for your project needs and marketing strategy, it is time to complete the documents you will use to market and sell your project. Once you have all your documents in hand, you will be ready to reach out to investors and raise capital.

THE USE OF ESCROW

Most EB-5 issuers promise in their offering documents to return an investor's subscription funds in the event the I-526 petition is denied. While there are currently no specific regulations requiring the use of an escrow, it has been widely adopted as a best practice to ensure that funds are available as promised.

What is an Escrow?

An escrow is a contractual arrangement formed and controlled by an escrow agreement made between two or more parties involved in a financial transaction. Practically speaking, one of the parties entrusts funds to an independent third party (the escrow agent) who receives, holds, and then disburses the money in satisfaction of mutually agreed-upon terms. Most often, the escrow agent is a bank, trust, or title company regulated by state or federal law. Some states have independent escrow companies as well, which provide only escrow services.

Escrows During the EB-5 Process

Escrows are used in the vast majority of EB-5 projects to receive the subscription funds from investors. Initial subscription funds are typically wired directly into a "subscription escrow account" pending release conditions related to the status of visa adjudication and sometimes other conditions. The proper use of escrow provides benefits to investors and issuers alike. From a financial perspective, a properly established escrow is a good way to assure the investor that his or her funds will be available for return should their I-526 be denied. A properly structured escrow also enables the development of a comprehensive audit trail of the investment. This is a critical component in providing evidence to support compliance with the immigration process.

Escrowing the investors' funds is as important to the capital raising process as it is to the immigration process. As a result, the escrow structure will have a significant impact on project marketability. While most EB-5 escrows terminate at the end of the I-526 adjudication process, they can also provide benefit during the development and/or settlement phases. This section focuses on the most common use of escrow in the EB-5 process—during the subscription phase.

Commonly Used Subscription Escrow Models

When escrow is used in the subscription phase of an offering, there are two basic models: "hold-until-approval" and "early-release".

Hold-Until-Approval. As the name implies, funds held under this structure remain in escrow until the corresponding investor's I-526 petition is approved. Upon receiving evidence of approval, the escrow agent releases the funds to the new commercial enterprise. This escrow is structured on an individual basis; each investor's $500,000 (or $1 million) investment is held in escrow until his or her particular I-526 petition is approved. The hold-until-approval model provides the highest level of funds security for investor protection because the funds are set aside and certain to be available for return if USCIS denies the investor's I-526 petition. While this model provides the highest level of funds security, it also means that it will take longer for the funds to be available to the EB-5 project. Remember that approval of investor petitions can take a year or more, and depending on when your investors subscribed to the project—all at once or staggering across months—you could be waiting extended amounts of time and/or only receiving the capital piecemeal. This often does not align with the realities of a construction budget and timetable.

Early-Release. An early-release escrow structure attempts to balance the security needs of the investor with the timing demands of capital for the project. There are several options for early-release that are commonly used, each with different levels of risk.

- **Release upon Filing:** In this model, funds are released from escrow once an investor's I-526 petition has been officially filed with USCIS. The escrow provides assurance to the investor that their immigration process has begun; however, it does not offer much other security. In the event of an I-526 denial, there is no guarantee that funds will be available to return the investor's subscription amount. Although this model improves the timing of deployment of funds, it creates significant risk for both investors and issuers (which may have already spent the funds needed to meet the contractual return obligation and may therefore fall into default).

- **Holdback/Reserve Account:** Another option is to use a holdback/reserve account where a portion of the overall capital raise is held to pay back investors that are denied. As a best practice, the holdback/reserve account should be set to accommodate the published USCIS denial rates. While this does not mitigate the risk of a complete project denial, it provides a likelihood that ample funds will be available to cover individual I-526 denials.

- **Hybrid:** Additional escrow structures can be created by combining elements of the early-release approach with the hold-until-approval approach. As an example, hold all funds until the first I-526 approval, and then release upon filing with a holdback/reserve account.

The best practice for early-release cases is to enable capital to be released into the new commercial enterprise in time to satisfy project deadlines, while at the same time providing the maximum assurance that funds will be available for return in the event of an investor denial or a complete project denial.

Impact of Escrow Terms on Project Funding

One recent study analyzed funding rates on more than 175 EB-5-related projects from within its client base to determine the impact of escrow use and structure on project funding. The results of the study showed a strong correlation between the security of the escrow structure and the length of time taken to fund the projects. In general, projects with more conservative escrow release terms (e.g., Hold-Until-Approval) funded better than those with more aggressive terms (e.g., Early-Release).

Another factor impacting the success of EB-5 capital raises is the track records of the parties involved. Given the recent surge of activity in the EB-5 sector, most projects are currently being promoted by new regional centers and developers without a significant track record of EB-5 specific projects. If you are new to the EB-5 game, the escrow structure plays a critical role in the investment decision and affects both the rate of funding for a project and the likelihood of achieving a full subscription. If you do not yet have a successful track record in EB-5, it may be best to go to market with the most conservative escrow terms possible to boost investors' confidence in the security of their investment.

In Summary

Establishing the right escrow solutions in EB-5 project offerings can give issuers a competitive advantage in the marketplace. When properly structured, the escrow appropriately balances the needs of investors and issuers in a way that maximizes the opportunity for project success and job creation, while minimizing the risk of financial loss for the investor.

EB-5 escrows are highly specialized and impact project success as well as immigration success. Accordingly, escrow planning is an integral part of developing an overall project offering. Issuers should begin planning well in advance of bringing their offerings to the market and consult early with experts in the field and escrow providers experienced in EB-5 to maximize marketability of their projects.

PREPARING YOUR PROJECT DOCUMENTS

Once you have decided how you plan to use investor funds, it is time to prepare the documents you will use to market your project to investors and demonstrate compliance with the program's regulations. These include corporate, transactional, disclosure, supporting, and marketing documents. In reviewing more about these documents below, keep in mind the constant tension among 1) making the project look as appealing as possible (for marketing benefits); 2) protecting the issuer from securities law liability for misstatements or omissions (particularly of investment risks); and 3) ensuring that no deal provisions (e.g., certain redemption rights), causes USCIS to reject EB-5 petitions based on these documents. Please note that steps set forth in *The EB-5 Handbook* should be used as a general guide rather than a do-it-yourself manual. Employing an experienced EB-5 team and designating a "quarterback" (as defined herein in this chapter) will not only increase efficiency and save you money, but will also increase your probability of success with the program.

The Offering Package

The offering package consists of documents you will present to investors and USCIS as part of investor visa petitions (I-526). The main goals of these documents are to structure and execute the deal, and also to carefully disclose the terms of the deal so the investor understands it clearly and accurately. An EB-5 offering package typically consists of:

- A short promotional document for the offering, known as a "teaser"
- Other marketing materials, such as web site descriptions
- A comprehensive private placement memorandum (detailed below)
- Subscription materials, including:
  - a detailed investor questionnaire addressing source of funds and securities law qualifications
  - a signature page or "joinder" to the limited partnership agreement or operating agreement
- Translations of these materials into the languages of the countries where the offering will be marketed

Now it is time to take a closer look at the private placement memorandum, which will make up the bulk of your offering package.

The Private Placement Memorandum

The private placement memorandum describes all aspects of the investment proposition. It is similar to a prospectus used in an initial public offering (IPO). Along with appropriate disclosures and disclaimers, a comprehensive private placement memorandum will typically include at least the following documentation:

- Limited partnership or limited liability company agreement (detailed below)
- Investment document representing the interest in the job-creating entity (loan, preferred equity, true equity, etc.)
- Escrow agreement (detailed below)

- Economist report
- Business plan
- Independent valuation reports
- Other project support materials
- Financial projections
- Construction budgets
- TEA designation letter

Partnership (or LLC) Agreements. The partnership (or LLC) agreement you prepare will establish the legal relationship between the issuer and the investors, and will be included with the private placement memorandum. The agreement details a number of things, including how the issuer will deploy investment dollars and the rights and responsibilities that investors are granted in exchange for their investment. Remember, in most situations the investor is investing in a new commercial enterprise that will then loan capital to the job-creating enterprise. The partnership agreements or operating agreements for EB-5 new commercial enterprises must address a number of legal considerations. These include:

- Provisions for the planned investment in the job-creating enterprise
- Provisions for alternative investments if the planned investment does not occur
- Escrow-related provisions
- Treatment of investors who do not apply for or receive approval of I-526s
- "Waterfall" provisions consistent with the investment proposition (for example, the preferred return and distributions on liquidation of the entity)
- Tax provisions
- Addressing multiple closings with respect to the visa process and investment into the job-creating enterprise
- Allocation of jobs created
- Management or policy-making rights of the limited partners, consistent with EB-5 program requirements
- Obligations of investors with respect to the visa application process
- Securities law qualifications of investors
- Transfer restrictions

Business Plan and Economic Report. You already learned about the business plan and economic report in *The EB-5 Handbook*. These two documents present your business model and how your project plans on creating the requisite jobs. Both investors and USCIS will want to see these documents to evaluate the job creation needed to support the visa petitions.

TEA Designation Letter. The TEA designation will be critical to the investors and project owners, because this letter determines whether the minimum investment level will be $500,000 or $1 million. As previously noted, TEA stands for targeted employment area and once designated, it decreases the minimum qualifying investment amount from $1 million to $500,000. To qualify as a TEA, the area in question must be either a rural area (a metropolitan statistical area having a population of less than 20,000) or an area where the unemployment level is 150 percent of the national average. Determining whether your project is or will be in a TEA is one of the earliest steps in establishing the feasibility of an EB-5 program. This is because it has been proven to be much more difficult to raise $1 million dollar investment amounts than $500,000.

Putting it All Together

Your EB-5 team of professionals prepares all of these documents with your input. You, as the project developer, will work with, at a minimum, the regional center (if you are not operating your own regional center), an economist, a business plan writer, an immigration lawyer, and a corporate/securities lawyer. You may also consult migration agents, broker-dealers, escrow agents, and translators.

The effort required to produce these materials is substantial. Quality EB-5 offering materials cannot be generated quickly based on templates. Experienced professionals will, of course, start with precedent material from prior offerings, but each project is different, and precedent material must be customized for every project.

All professionals must perform their functions with a high degree of care and attention to the latest developments in USCIS adjudication policy, securities laws and other laws, and market expectations. If you lack the experience or capacity to quarterback all of these professionals, one of them will need to serve as quarterback for the whole process. The professionals must also coordinate with each other, and if any one professional lacks skill, experience or bandwidth, it will negatively affect the other professionals and the quality and legal protections of the offering materials.

Either the immigration lawyer or corporate lawyer will typically quarterback the overall process, playing a large role in preparation of these materials. They work with the team ensuring the documentation (e.g., offering documents, loan agreements, economic reports, etc.) does not violate USCIS rules and policies. The relative roles vary significantly for each project, though.

How Long Does it Take and How Much Coes it Cost? These questions are critical to project developers, and EB-5 professionals must answer them for every new client. Unfortunately, the answers are rarely as simple as new clients wish they would be. In general, EB-5 has higher upfront costs than other forms of financing. The documents are labor intensive and require a well thought-out structure, much of which is executed by attorneys. Both timing and cost for completion of offering materials depend on many factors. For example, all of the following factors might impact the timing and cost for developing these materials: type of project (direct vs. indirect); industry, including industry-specific risks; availability and quality of existing disclosure on the project; whether due diligence will be performed and who will perform it; availability and quality of offering documents used by the developer or regional center for prior projects; non-EB-5 capital structure; relationship of the project developer and the regional center, including the terms of any agreement between them; how the project will be marketed (migration agents, broker-dealers, which countries, etc.); EB-5 investment terms, including investment type, return, subordination, security, escrow terms, etc.; project-specific risks; and skill, experience and bandwidth of the other EB-5 professionals.

Most often, many of these factors are undetermined when the request for timing and cost quotes are first made. Certain parts of the offering package, such as the economist report, are more predictable and can more easily be quoted for time and cost after a brief client interview. Other parts, such as the private placement memorandum and the limited partnership or operating agreement, cannot be accurately quoted for time or cost without extensive discussions with the client about the design of the offering, including all the factors listed above.

Some firms address these uncertainties by providing for fixed or not-to-exceed quotes based on extensive assumptions and limitations. Those quotes will ultimately be only as accurate as are the assumptions and limitations. The lowest quotes will likely have assumptions and limitations that exclude work that is required for a quality, legally compliant offering, such as program design, advice and execution on securities law compliance, due diligence on factual information in the offering memorandum and/or "running the deal."

Some law firms and professionals ask for relatively modest initial payments for project planning and feasibility, and from such work, the firm can produce an accurate quote for the preparation of all parts of the offering package that the firm will prepare.

Differing quotation practices can make it difficult for a developer to predict the true costs and timing to produce a quality EB-5 offering package, particularly if the developer wishes not to pay for initial project planning and feasibility analysis. The developer in this position is akin to a developer seeking accurate time and cost quotes from construction contractors before obtaining architectural plans.

To obtain accurate time and cost estimates for a quality EB-5 offering package, you should:

1. Choose a single "quarterback" for the project. The quarterback should be highly skilled and experienced and should be well-networked in the EB-5 community. The quarterback is normally a law firm, but other professionals could serve in this role. If the "quarterback" is not an EB-5- experienced corporate/securities law firm or immigration law firm, the project may be fundamentally flawed from the beginning, significantly delaying the project and increasing costs as subsequently hired corporate/securities lawyers and immigration lawyers do extra work to try to salvage or repair substandard or imprudent initial work.

2. Allow the quarterback to refer other professionals it knows and trusts. If there is any fee-sharing for such referrals, you should demand full disclosure. (Most quality law firms do not share fees with any other professionals.)

3. Before relying on quotes from professionals who do not know what others are doing, allow the quarterback to define all of the work required for a successful offering package and divide such work among your internal staff, the regional center, and the various professionals.

4. Choose professionals appropriate for the nature of the work. Experience with past EB-5 projects is a good indicator of quality or success in today's market, but far from the only indicator, given the rapidly evolving marketplace and increasingly demanding legal, due diligence, and quality standards.

5. Do not assume that you or your regional center will do work it has never done before and has no dedicated resources to perform. Too often, developers believe they can, for example, draft an EB-5 business plan, but they have neither the experience nor the available personnel to do so. Self-producing late or inferior work product will cause delay and increase your costs for the professionals who must ultimately perform or redo such work.

6. Be willing to pay modest amounts for the "architectural" work that can be

involved in producing an accurate time and cost estimate. That work needs to be done anyway for a successful offering, and professionals who do that work will charge for it one way or another. (Please note the emphasis on successful—a number of projects fail in the marketplace because of factors that were easily predictable up front).

7. Be wary of lowball quotes. Professional firms in like quality tiers have similar internal cost structures and will take roughly the same amount of time to do the same work. Big differences in quotes should be questioned. Perhaps one firm believes the scope of work will be substantially greater than another firm. Why is that? Perhaps the lower quoting firm plans to devote only its lower cost (i.e., more junior) resources to the work. Is that what you want, or will you expect to have ready access to the higher level of competence and experience of more senior talent?

8. If a firm is willing to bid the project at what seems to be a loss (giving scope of work and promised resources), consider what type of service and quality is incentivized by that arrangement.

As of this writing, when a project is properly scoped and bid, the result will typically be one to three months to prepare offering materials, and a total cost of all professionals of between $100,000 and $200,000. These guidelines do not include the work for a new I-924 regional center designation. Also, many factors can lead to greater time or greater cost (or occasionally, less time and less cost). No rules of thumb can take the place of detailed consultations about your project with knowledgeable professionals. The good news is that for a successful EB-5 raise of even moderate size (e.g., $10 million or more), even the highest end of the cost spectrum will be dwarfed by the cost of capital savings you will achieve by using EB-5 compared with other available financing in the same risk tier.

MARKETING YOUR PROJECT

Once you have your project documents in hand, it is time to begin selling your project to investors. By now you understand the importance of marketing and catering to what EB-5 investors are looking for. It is now time to dig deeper into strategy.

The question most new projects face is: What do I need to do to promote an EB-5 investment? Most EB-5 projects begin the same way: by completing all of the offering and project documents, and generating marketing materials. When preparing marketing materials, there are a few fundamental lessons that should be kept in mind. First is the question of whether to translate the documents into the investor's own language. One school of thought is that doing so increases the

Tip

Is the project located in a TEA and is the TEA letter current? The TEA letter must be updated yearly to ensure that the amount to be invested is $500,000 (the TEA amount). Also, USCIS has stated somewhat murkily in its Adjudicators Field Manual that if there is an escrow provision, the date the I-526 is submitted is the date that USCIS looks to for determining whether the project is located in a TEA. Because USCIS's position seems to conflict with the EB-5 regulations, the Foreign Affairs Manual, and other sources of law, be sure to discuss this issue with your immigration lawyer to ensure you understand USCIS's latest approach if your project is being funded near the end of the validity period of your project's TEA letter).

effectiveness of the disclosures (providing greater legal protection to the issuer) and avoids translations performed by others that you cannot control. Another school of thought is that doing so is costly and makes the issuer potentially liable for errors in translation and meaning. This is an important issue to discuss with your corporate/securities firm and your marketing professionals.

Second, most developers are familiar with generating hard copy marketing materials, but EB-5 projects should keep in mind the differences between conventional investment audiences and potential EB-5 investors. The priorities of EB-5 investors are distinctly different: traditional investment audiences focus largely on financial elements of a project, including both return of capital and expected rate of return, whereas EB-5 investors prioritize likelihood of immigration success and secondarily return of capital, with little concern for rate of return. Therefore, EB-5 marketing materials will have a heavy emphasis on how the project complies with essential elements of the EB-5 visa program (e.g. TEA certification, job creation, regional center approval, and escrow mechanics)—elements that are absent in traditional investment marketing materials.

Moving the Offering Overseas

With offering and marketing materials in hand, the developer will not need to venture overseas. Many countries offer companies that specialize in international migration and can offer your project as a means of pursuing an EB-5 visa. There are some general considerations on evaluating how much time you should spend overseas during the capital raise.

One such consideration is that issuers are responsible for the messages about the offering communicated to potential investors. Offerings are typically communicated via seminars to groups of investors or individually in face-to-face discussions. The more time members of the project spend overseas, the better they will be able to articulate and accurately convey important project details.

Another valid consideration in how much time a project should spend overseas is maintaining the interest of the overseas investors. "Out of sight, out of mind" prevails in the EB-5 marketplace like everywhere else, and without follow-up to a brief trip overseas, interest in your project could be replaced by interest in some other project. Also, without some sort of follow-up presence, potential investors may have additional questions but decide not to pursue them because the investor finds international communication troublesome or too impersonal.

By offering face-to-face interaction with project principals, the project may benefit from earning additional credibility. Many projects offer biographies of key principals, but resumes or background on paper may prove to be less effective than an opportunity to meet project principals in person and ask questions about the project that foreign representatives, less familiar with development, cannot answer as well. Personal relationships are key with many overseas investors and face-to-face interaction may provide considerably more value than corporate logos, photos, as-built renderings, or summaries of past successes (many of which appear in all EB-5 projects).

Finally, sustained overseas travel or presence permits the project principals more opportunities for EB-5 investors to ask questions, not only about the project, but about the immigration process or life in general in the United States. Certainly, investors are going to have questions about the document-heavy procedures involved with EB-5, such as the documentation related to the project (e.g., private placement memorandum, business plan, partnership (or LLC) agreements, etc.), but they also ask questions related to proving the lawfulness of their sources of funds. The United States government (USCIS) requires extensive documentation verifying the investor's investment comes from lawful sources. For many, this can be a very personal subject, and having a friendly, caring face to answer questions regarding the necessity and the sufficiency of these documents can be an appealing option for a potential investor.

Compliance

Any competent discussion of promoting EB-5 investment requires an acknowledgement of the necessity of compliance with US securities laws. While some in the industry disagree, representatives for the Securities and Exchange Commission (SEC) have consistently stated that syndicated EB-5 investments are securities, and the offer and sale of such investments, even though to foreign nationals, is subject to the same securities laws applicable to offers and sales of other securities. While there are certain exemptions from certain compliance obligations available for foreign activities, they are technical and heavily conditioned, and never apply to allegations that disclosure was erroneous or misleading. Despite recent reforms to US securities laws that relax certain rules regarding the promotion of investments, it is mandatory to consult with experts in securities law concerning your EB-5 marketing campaign. Recent events and statements from federal agencies, including the SEC, have indicated that EB-5 offerings are a topic of increasing interest and focus (see Chapter 11). The formerly prevailing view that EB-5 offerings were somehow immune from the laws and practices (and consequences of non-compliance) that apply in other offerings was simply wrong and no longer prevails. Following best practices for securities offerings serves both you and the investors well in the long run and there is no need or good reason to cut corners because your offering is EB-5.

WORKING WITH MIGRATION AGENTS

The most important step in the capital raise process is reaching investors. In China, the largest EB-5 market, projects, and regional centers typically work with migration agents to promote their projects to investors. For legal and cultural reasons, it is quite difficult for projects to sell directly to investors in the Chinese market. You should be wary of those who claim they "have connections" and can locate investors in China without migration agents. There is a significant chance such persons will be unable to fill even a moderately-sized offering, leaving you with the bills for your up-front costs and not enough capital to complete your project.

What is a Migration Agent?

EB-5 marketing is unusual in that—unlike agents in the United States who sell securities and must be licensed as broker-dealers by the U.S. Securities and Exchange Commission (SEC)—agents in many countries overseas finding investors for EB-5 securities are not experts in securities, but are instead experts in helping individuals and families migrate out of the home country. In addition, to the extent they are licensed at all, such agents are not licensed as securities agents but as "migration" agents.

Agents charge a range of fee amounts and fee types. It is best to discuss fees with each specific migration agency. The largest fee is typically a major portion of the "administrative fee" that EB-5 projects charge EB-5 investors. Agents may also charge the investor directly for providing the agent's own administrative services, which can include document preparation, translation, and so on.

Finding an Agency

In years past, it was difficult to find out who the migration agents were overseas, and those with access to such agents charged handsomely for making

Tip

When project developers sell projects in China, marketing strategy is very important. Before investing any money in marketing a project, developers should do their homework.

To this end, prior to selling the project, developers should visit a number of agencies in China to better understand the local market, such as referral fees, service charges, and other related issues. Working closely with an agency at the beginning stages of marketing with help developers avoid unnecessary costs. Typically, developers or their intermediary should visit at least 10 to 20 agencies shortly before commencing the offering to understand the current market conditions.

introduction to agents. It is now becoming much easier to find out who the agents actually are, although it can still be difficult for developers and regional centers to successfully navigate agent recruiting. In addition to issues of geographic, time zone, cultural, and language barriers, there are now far more projects and regional centers competing for investors than in previous years and market conditions (including offering terms) are constantly shifting.

Presenting Project Materials

Even though real estate developers and regional centers are facing tough competition in the EB-5 capital market with new projects being presented to the Chinese investment marketplace on a daily basis, many of these projects are not considered attractive and sellable when first presented to a migration agent. First impressions are very important in the EB-5 market, as migration agents are often far too busy to help project developers improve their marketing materials. It is the developer's or regional center's responsibility to create eye-catching, informative, and accurate project documents to increase the chances for a successful partnership. There are certain guidelines that all EB-5 projects should follow when presenting to migration agents.

The project documents should be specific to the particular project and include enough details to paint a vivid picture. Though documentation should be detailed, the project developer or regional center should not plan on submitting all their information to the agents during an introductory contact or meeting. A more practical and appealing way to present your project to agents is through a slide show presentation that highlights the most important details of your project. Such details should include the background and track record of the developers/regional center involved, the proposed capital stack for the project, and the exit strategy. Additional information may be included as it relates to specifics or exclusive benefits of the project.

The Capital Stack. The capital stack presentation should include information such as the portion of developer equity and whether the project is being structured as debt or equity. The ratio of EB-5 funds and developer equity is also a critical factor. An attractive project will have significant developer equity and not rely solely on EB-5 funding and debt financing to support the project (See Chapter 7). The best projects are those that do not necessarily *need* EB-5 funding to proceed.

A project's total equity should be based upon the appraised value of the project in three variations: the existing asset valuation; the completed project value; and the stabilized value. An independent third-party appraisal of the project should be included and this information should be featured to help the migration agents assess the overall strength of the project.

Exit Strategy. The exit strategy is one of the most important issues EB-5 investors will examine when reviewing a potential investment opportunity. For most EB-5 investors, receiving permanent residency and getting their money back are the two most important concerns when investing. A migration agent will place a great deal of importance on the exit strategy and how a project is realistically going to pay back the investors (See Chapter 3). Failure to include contemplated exit strategies in the initial marketing material will draw concerns from an experienced migration agent.

Reviewing Marketability. Additional information from the developer must be included in the initial marketing summary to allow migration agents to review a project's marketability. The materials should list any guarantees that the developer can offer to the new commercial enterprise, such as construction guarantees. If a project is counting mostly indirect construction jobs and then offers a construction guarantee, agents are more likely to believe that the jobs will actually be created. Feasibility reports are also critical for projects, as USCIS is requiring more and more information to be validated by independent third parties.

Tip

For inexperienced developers and EB-5 regional centers, it is always wise to approach the migration agents for comments and suggestions before the project is finalized and opportunities to restructure are limited or prohibitively expensive. What seems attractive in a general developing sense may not be so attractive when it comes to EB-5 investments. What may seem like a safe investment in the regular financing world may create an undesirable investment for EB-5 investors. Even the capital structures and investment terms that sold a year or even six months ago may not sell today.

A project must pass through the initial basic review and meet different standards before it can be recommended for a comprehensive, in-depth review. Lastly, it is important to remember that developers and regional centers should have their information solidified before serious discussions can proceed. These guidelines will provide a good template, but make sure you are working with a qualified EB-5 team to structure project materials in a way that will appeal to migration agents and investors.

Finally, please note that historically the Chinese Exit-Entry Bureau requires licensing for any agencies promoting EB-5 in China, although the central government seems to be experimenting with loosening the licensing requirements to allow easier approaches to licensing. Nonetheless, developers and regional centers should verify the licensure of all migration agents before entering into agreement to avoid any unnecessary legal issues.

Do I Have to Use a Migration Agent? Although migration agents certainly play an important role in the EB-5 investor process, there are other ways to locate investors. As simplistic as it sounds, a good website that has clear information and transparency is very helpful (though always consult with securities counsel before marketing EB-5 investments on your website). Also, speaking with financial advisors and other professionals that work with high net worth individuals can assist in making contacts with potential investors. Finally, arranging seminars in foreign countries to discuss EB-5 and the regional center project can help create an awareness of the program and possibilities for investors should they have greater interest. It seems that there are many underserved, less mature markets that could be valuable markets for the EB-5 program. Regional centers and project developers might consider investing time and resources in those areas in addition to China. Regardless of the method used to identify potential investors, there is a large gap between simply identifying someone who may be interested in an EB-5 investment and actually closing the investment. As a developer, you may have already experienced this in raising traditional capital; it is no less a concern in EB-5.

SECURITIES ISSUES RELATED TO SOLICITING INVESTORS

In addition to being successful from a marketing perspective, syndicated EB-5 offerings need to comply with US securities laws governing such offerings. Therefore, regional centers and project developers need to ensure that they comply with such rules and how they apply to the EB-5 offering.

As mentioned in prior sections, foreign nationals making an EB-5 investment usually receive, in exchange for their investment, either:

- a limited partnership interest in a limited partnership, or
- a membership interest in a limited liability company.

As noted above, the SEC takes the view that the interests in these entities, or what you are "selling" to investors, are securities under US securities laws. These interests may also be considered securities under the laws of many of the foreign countries in which EB-5 investors reside. Because EB-5 offerings are considered securities, US securities laws and regulations require that certain conditions are met when you are promoting projects and accepting investments. These laws and regulations are designed to ensure that investors are as informed as possible when they decide to invest in your project.

No developer should be deterred from considering EB-5 capital simply because EB-5 investments involve securities laws. Decades of traditions exist as to how to properly conduct foreign, syndicated offerings of project or investment fund interests. Many law firms and individual lawyers specialize in these matters and many investment professionals operate comfortably in compliance with them. General expertise in investment fund formation and securities offerings is available at many quality law firms, even though the specific expertise deploying these laws and traditions in the EB-5 context is relatively scarce at this time.

What Does it Mean That EB-5 Investments Are Considered Securities?

First, it means that the investment opportunity is subject to laws requiring either, on the one hand, registration or qualification, or, on the other hand, an available exemption from registration or qualification. Under all US and state securities laws, registration/qualification is the default if no exemption is

Tip

Promoting Securities: Since September 2013, general solicitation – that is, advertising, public web sites, open seminars and the like–has been permitted for Rule 506 offerings so long as the purchasers are all verified accredited investors. (Accredited investors include individuals with at least $1 million in net worth, excluding equity in their home, or $200,000 of annual income [$300,000 with spouse]). A qualified corporate/securities attorney should be consulted to ensure that your project meets the qualifications of Rule 506.

available or if the conditions of the exemption were not satisfied. Fortunately, exemptions are typically available for all US and state securities laws as long as the offerings are structured and executed properly with these exemptions in mind. The typical exemptions used for EB-5 are Regulation S for offerings to non-US persons and Regulation D for private placements. Many offerings rely on both. Offerings under Rule 506 of Regulation D have the added benefit of being automatically exempt from state qualification requirements, which can be difficult for EB-5 programs to comply with.

Second, those who locate and introduce eligible investors have to consider whether their activities require registration under the broker-dealer laws of the United States and any state in which they conduct these activities. To date, most EB-5 capital has been raised without the assistance of registered broker-dealers. However, the threat of enforcement action by regulators and the risks to project developers and regional centers from using unlicensed "marketing agents" and "finders" are setting the stage for increasing involvement of licensed broker-dealers in the EB-5 industry. As of this writing, several licensed broker-dealer firms are active in the marketing of EB-5 investments.

Third, regional centers or developers that serve as manager or general partner of the new commercial enterprise must consider if their activities require registration under federal or state law as an investment adviser. The Dodd-Frank Wall Street Reform and Consumer Protection Act, adopted in 2010, made significant changes to the investment adviser laws which resulted in many managers of private funds becoming registered investment advisers under federal or state law. Registration entails record-keeping requirements and can also result in limits on the type of compensation that advisers can receive. This is a complicated and specialized area of law, and developers and regional centers that act as managers or general partners should consult with experienced investment adviser counsel for each project to ensure the availability of exemptions or compliance.

Fourth, the new commercial enterprise may be considered an investment company, and investment companies are subject to registration requirements unless there is an available exemption. The operating and reporting requirements for registered investment companies (such as mutual funds) are typically incompatible with new commercial enterprises in an EB-5 program. Accordingly, a conclusion that the new commercial enterprise is not an investment company or that it meets a registration exemption is required for a legally compliant EB-5 program. The easiest and most common exemption to rely upon is the "3(c)(1) exemption," which exempts any investment company that has 100 or fewer investors. This means that an EB-5 project which raises no more than $50 million in a $500,000 program will have a ready exemption available.

Ultimately compliance is important, because the penalties for non-compliance with securities laws are severe. However, compliance is almost always achievable by simply selecting qualified and experienced professionals and allowing these professionals a realistic scope of work and budget comparable to what they do for non-EB-5 offerings. As noted above, the cost savings of EB-5 compared to other forms of capital in like risk tiers generally dwarf the modest extra cost of experienced legal professionals empowered to perform a full scope of work. Compromising on the experience and reputation of legal professionals selected, or selecting the right professionals, but clipping their wings through constrained scopes of work, are penny-wise and pound-foolish in the EB-5 arena.

CHAPTER 10: WHAT ARE MY RESPONSIBILITIES AFTER THE CAPITAL RAISE?

By Linda Lau, Joseph McCarthy, and Reid Thomas

After you have successfully raised the EB-5 capital you need for your project, it is time to turn to proper administration of the funds you have been entrusted with. Remember that, unlike traditional development projects, your investors are relying on your EB-5 project to help them meet their immigration goals. Because of this, you need to pay close attention to how you are meeting the goals that you laid out when your investors subscribed to the project.

At this point your investors—provided all EB-5 requirements have been met—will be conditional permanent residents with temporary green cards. It is not until they can prove to USCIS—through an I-829 petition—that their investment created or is likely to create within a reasonable time, 10 U.S. jobs, that conditions will be removed on their residency and they will receive *permanent* green cards. This is where you come in. Among other things, as the developer it is important that you are meeting key milestones: sticking to your business plan, using investor funds appropriately, and creating at least 10 jobs per investor.

As you learned in earlier chapters, second to receiving their permanent green card, investors place a high importance on having their original investment returned to them. Because of this, returning investor funds is a mark of a successful project. In this chapter you will discover tips on fund administration, the evidence you will need to provide for investors' I-829 petitions to remove conditions on their permanent residency, and some common methods used to return investor funds.

EB-5 FUND ADMINISTRATION

Proper administration of the EB-5 funds is essential to the efficient operation of the new commercial enterprise and the regional center and the success of a project. The complexities of administration are inherent in the program itself. The funds come from foreign individuals, and there are multiple stakeholders involved, such as the investor, his/her family members, attorneys, advisors, and brokers. In addition, there are complex US banking laws and US government requirements that must be navigated.

It is important to implement an effective and efficient fund administration solution from the beginning of the subscription process, or operational costs and compliance risk may increase substantially, thereby reducing or even eliminating the cost advantage of the EB-5 capital.

Selecting an outside EB-5 fund administrator is an option issuers may want to consider. This is a common best practice used by many managers of more traditional investment funds—e.g., pension funds, hedge funds, etc. Unlike some of these heavily regulated funds, there is no requirement in EB-5 to use a third-party administrator. Nonetheless, using one is becoming a more common practice because of the additional security and transparency it brings to investors.

Although there may be similarities between the administration of EB-5 funds and other types of funds, there are also many unique issues that require a high degree of expertise and specialization. For issuers, the proper setup of an EB-5 specific fund administration process or selection of an EB-5 fund administrator is key to achieving their business objectives.

The EB-5 immigration process is lengthy and complex. It lasts between four to five years for a typical investor, and the compliance rules and industry regulations are frequently in flux. Proper planning and implementation of a fund administration solution from the beginning can make the difference between a successful or unsuccessful result for the issuer and for the investor.

Meeting Investor Objectives

From the EB-5 investor's perspective, the reward of proper fund administration and a successful project is permanent residency and the end game is the successful adjudication of their I-829 petition. You are best served by planning well in advance for the filing of investors' I-829 petitions and establishing their fund administration solution prior to the capital raise phase. With I-526 processing times included, there may be over two years' worth of operational and financial tracking and documentation necessary to substantiate the evidence required for investors' I-829 petitions. Without proper retention and recording, compiling the requisite information to complete the I-829 can be extremely time consuming, expensive, and risky. Submitting an incomplete or late petition puts the immigration result at risk.

In order to mitigate this risk, you should work with qualified EB-5 professionals—whether you outsource completely or work with the individual professionals that you have already assembled as part of your team. When preparing the project documents needed to support your investors' I-829 petitions, do not rely on guesswork or beginner's luck.

The I-829 Petition. The I-829 Petition by Entrepreneur to Remove Conditions accomplishes exactly what the name suggests: removes conditions on the investor's permanent residency. In simpler terms, USCIS uses the evidence provided with this form to determine whether or not the investor actually met the requirements of the EB-5 program as established in his or her I-526 petition. The I-829 petition must include evidence that:

- The commercial enterprise was established. USCIS suggests that such evidence may include, but is not limited to:
  - Entity formation documents or certificates of good standing
  - Complete list of investors/owners in the enterprise
  - Federal income tax returns
  - Progress updates provided to investors
  - Bank statements for the new commercial enterprise over the entire period
- The foreign investor invested the requisite capital. Such evidence may include:
  - An audited financial statement
  - Copies of the investor's executed subscription agreement
  - Bank statements showing the transfer of the full amount of funds from the escrow account into the commercial enterprise
- The full capital investment was continually maintained at risk in the commercial enterprise over the entire two-year period of conditional residence. Acceptable evidence, as required by USCIS, may include:
  - Monthly bank statements
  - Copies of investment statements to investors throughout the period
  - Invoices or receipts showing funds applied to the project
  - Federal or state income tax returns
- 10 full-time jobs have already been or are expected to be created within a reasonable time frame:
  - Monthly bank statements for commercial enterprise showing payroll
  - Tax returns or Form I-9

- Receipts that correlate investment to the business plan and economist's report

The documents are simple enough, but they will rely on months, if not years, of your careful preparation and close consultation with seasoned EB-5 experts. If USCIS is satisfied with the evidence you provide (and with the rest of the investor's petition) your investor will have conditions removed on his or her conditional residence, receive a permanent green card.

Planning Ahead

The ideal foundation for an effective fund administration solution is proper escrow account setup and management. The escrow agreement and controls put in place by the escrow agent provide a natural starting point for a comprehensive audit trail.

From that point on, it is crucial to track the deployment of funds into the project as outlined in the applicable business plan to ensure compliance with USCIS requirements and ultimately prepare for the completion and filing of the I-829 petition.

Issuers should evaluate delivering these services in-house compared to hiring a third-party fund administrator. While there is no regulatory requirement today to use an independent third-party fund administrator for EB-5, it is increasingly being adopted and considered a best practice. Independent of regulatory requirements, however, a third-party fund administrator provides an additional layer of security and transparency for investors. Continual increases in the levels of security, transparency, and compliance end up benefiting all stakeholders in the EB-5 industry.

<u>RETURN OF FUNDS</u>

An EB-5 investor does not consider his or her effort a success until two things happen: 1) USCIS approves the I-829 petition to remove conditions, so the investor and family members receive permanent, unconditional green cards; and 2) the new commercial enterprise returns his or her capital.

Most loans—remember, investments are typically injected into the project as a loan to the job-creating enterprise—in the EB-5 context are typically 60 months (five years), though some may be six or more years. In addition, most such loans, whether the initial term is five or six years or more, typically also have at least one or two optional extension periods. At first, such terms seem long when the investor's conditional green card period is only two years long. When looking such loans more carefully in the EB-5 context, the seemingly long loan periods make more sense, both for the developer and for the EB-5 investor.

Why a 60-Month Loan?

All EB-5 business plans should contemplate from the outset—without guarantees—eventual return of capital to the investor. Because investors place a high level of importance on receiving their initial investment back, investments are typically deployed to the project in the form of a loan to the job-creating entity. This structure allows for the investor to meet the "at risk" requirement of the program while still maintaining an interest in the business that has a higher priority than equity alone. The regulations require that investments be "continuously maintained" throughout the investor's two-year conditional residency period. If investors are so keen to get their funds back and the regulations only require an investment period of two years, why are most EB-5 investments held for five years?

The logic behind five-year loans can be seen a little more clearly when comparing the potential timing spread among all EB-5 investors in the project from the fastest to the slowest. As mentioned in the escrow section, release of each EB-5 investor's capital from escrow to the new commercial enterprise (which then makes the money potentially available to be loaned to the "job-creating enterprise") might be conditioned in one of several ways, such as holding until each I-526 petition is approved, holding until a certain number of I-526 petitions are approved, or holding for certain other triggers. For the example below, however, let's assume that all EB-5 capital is released upon the first I-526 approval. Let's also assume that the first I-526 is approved on April 1, 2014, and the loan is made. That means that the first investor (whose I-526 was approved) can now either apply to receive his or her visa in the home country or adjust status to conditional resident in the United States. The consular process takes at least six months, which means that the first investor is eligible to enter the United States on October 1, 2014. Nonetheless, the investor actually has six months to enter on this visa, and many do not enter on the very first day, so let's assume the first investor enters three months after immigrant visa issuance. That would be January 1, 2015. In turn, the first investor would be eligible to file the I-829 on October 1, 2016 (3 months before the two-year anniversary of his or her residence). Given that I-829 adjudication is now taking at least nine months, the earliest that the first investor could theoretically receive his or her investment back would be June 2017. This overall timeframe by itself would require that the loan be at least 38 months long.

The need for a loan longer than that, however, is because many other investors in the project might take longer to prepare and file their I-526 and I-829 petitions, and those petitions may run into problems or delays, or other unexpected problems and delays may arise along the way. For example, it is possible that the second investor files six months or more after the first investor, and it is also possible that the second investor encounters issues that cause his or her I-526 petition to take an additional six months. Then when the I-526 petition is finally approved, the second investor might take the full six months allowed before actually entering the United States. This could cause the second investor to arrive a year and half or more after the first investor (entry starts the two-year clock on the investor's conditional residency period). Assuming other investors could similarly run into problems and delays along the way, it could easily be 60 months before the final investor obtains his or her I-829 approval. All things considered, a 60-month loan accounts for the timing realities of the EB-5 program.

Repayment of the Loan vs. Repayment of Capital

It is important to note that the loan is not directly from the EB-5 investor, but instead from the new commercial enterprise to the job-creating enterprise. That creates the possibility that the job-creating enterprise might pay the loan back to the new commercial enterprise before all EB-5 investors have obtained their I-829 removal-of-conditions approvals. This creates an issue of whether EB-5 investors who still have not obtained I-829 approval nonetheless remain in compliance with the regulations and USCIS policies that their investment be maintained throughout their conditional permanent residency.

Arguably, from the investor's perspective, the money is still "at risk" because it is still in the hands of the new commercial enterprise. Additionally, the required jobs have already been created by the prior infusion of the loan proceeds into the project where the funds were used to purchase job-creating goods and services. The question of whether USCIS will agree that such post-repayment holding of funds by the new commercial enterprise qualifies as the investment being continuously maintained remains. Because the qualification of "continuously maintained" relates to the investor's investment in the new commercial enterprise, and not the relationship between the new commercial enterprise and the job-creating enterprise, it seems logical that the money should still be considered at risk. Unfortunately, USCIS has not yet clarified this issue. In the meantime, this remains a grey area and since USCIS has not provided policy guidance, if a developer wanted to repay the loan from the new commercial enterprise early, under no scenario should the new commercial enterprise distribute the capital to the investors. Instead, developers should hold the funds within the new commercial enterprise and repay investors only upon receipt of their I-829 approval.

Loan Extensions

As mentioned above, many loans in EB-5 include one or more potential term extensions (at borrower's option), typically in one-year increments and commonly with the penalty that the interest rate increases. From a developer's perspective, however, such loan extensions, even if technically allowed under the applicable loan agreement, should be carefully considered before being exercised—particularly if the developer wants to use EB-5 funding again in the future. Specifically, if the developer exercises the loan extension option, investors may feel that the return of their money has been unreasonably delayed—even if such options to extend the loan are in fact included in the loan documentation. In any event, the developer would be wise to maintain constant communication with its investors as to the status of the project and possible loan repayment in the near future, so if an extension is ever needed, the investors will have some specific, timely warnings, which can help them make plans for the delayed return of funds.

CONCLUSION

At this point you have learned the basics of the EB-5 program and how to determine if EB-5 capital is the right choice for your project. Once you have decided to embark on the EB-5 capital raising journey, you'll structure your capital stack and decide how you plan on accepting EB-5 investments—directly or through a regional center (and if through a regional center, in what capacity). When your project plans are finalized, you'll make sure all the necessary documents are in order, including your offering documents and you'll iron out your marketing strategy. After all that preparation, you're ready to reach out to investors and accept investments. Whether you work with migration agents or recruit investors using other strategies, this is the point when you will begin to see the fruits of your labor. But, as you know, your work is not over yet. Investors will need to file their I-526 petitions, and upon approval, their investment funds will become available to your project. As they are waiting out their conditional permanent residency period, you'll need to make sure that you are properly administering their funds and sticking to your business plan. At the end of their two-year conditional residency, investors will be looking to you for the evidence that they fulfilled the conditions of the EB-5 program—namely that their investment created at least 10 jobs. To come full circle, after your investors receive their permanent green cards, you'll return their funds and reap the rewards of the EB-5 program—a completed development project, new jobs for US workers, and immigration opportunities for foreign investors, all, as they say in the business, at no cost to the US taxpayer.

CHAPTER 11: THE FUTURE OF EB-5
By Joseph McCarthy

These are exciting times in the world of EB-5, as participation in the program is booming. EB-5 has proven to be a popular option as a capital source (for qualified projects) in the wake of the global financial crash of 2008. With its increased use, however, developers and immigrants alike are seeing the program as one way to accomplish their goals.

NAVIGATING A GROWING PROGRAM

In 2013, the number of EB-5 visas issued grew to an all-time high of 8,564[1], up from just over 1,400 in 2008, only five years prior. Likewise, the number of entities creating and using regional centers has similarly increased. Around 2007, the number of USCIS-approved regional centers was 16; by 2013, the number of approved regional centers exceeded 400.

The Rocky Trajectory

The past six years of the EB-5 program are a stark contrast to the 18 years prior. The program remained relatively unknown during most of the first two decades of its existence and, accordingly, the number of visas issued was a small fraction of the 10,000 visas allocated annually for the program. The program fell fall short of its potential, and the corresponding potential of billions of dollars of capital influx to the US economy. Indeed, the success of the program for the first 20 years was disappointing compared to its aspirations. According to a 2005 Government Accountability Office (GAO) study analyzing State Department records, a total of only 6,024 visas had been issued to immigrant investors and their dependents in the 15 years since the start of the program. In 2012 alone, the State Department issued 7,641 EB-5 visas, and even issued a warning that the quota for Chinese investors might be reached in fiscal year 2013[2].

Coping with Rapid Growth

The EB-5 program has grown so rapidly in the past few years that a great deal of attention is starting to be paid to the 10,000-visa cap, and the likelihood that the

1.   The 8,564 figure includes visas issued at foreign services posts abroad and adjustments of status made in the United States under the EB-5 visa program in 2013. In 2008, the figure was 1,443. See U.S. Department of State. *Report of the Visa Office 2013; Report of the Visa Office 2008.*
2.   U.S. Department of State. *Visa Bulletin for December 2012.*

number of EB-5 investors will exceed the cap within the next 12 to 24 months. This concern has led many EB-5 professionals and trade associations to propose a number of legislative solutions to Congress, including increasing the allocation of visas for the program and not counting derivative visas (those issued to the EB-5 investor's spouse and dependents) against the 10,000-visa cap. So far, no investors have been waitlisted, but with the keen interest in the program and existing per-country numerical visa limitations, it remains a very real possibility.

Rapid growth of the program has also placed greater administrative and professional burdens on USCIS in terms of reviewing and processing the increasing number of EB-5 petitions, including most prominently, regional center applications (I-924), individual investor petitions (I-526), and individual investor petitions for removal of permanent residency conditions (I-829). USCIS has taken strides to manage the volume of increasing and frequently complex applications, petitions and cases, and to respond to new program challenges by increasing the sophistication and number of EB-5 personnel at USCIS. USCIS also has to deal with increased scrutiny of legislators and interrelated federal agencies as a result of unfavorable press coverage of the program due to actions of a few bad actors in the EB-5 community (e.g., the complaint filed in 2013 by the Securities and Exchange Commission against A Chicago Convention Center, LLC). The increased attention caused by these controversies seems to actually have created an unexpected benefit, as seen in the increasing communication, cooperation, and collaboration among USCIS, other federal agencies, lawmakers and stakeholders. These collective efforts have resulted in great strides toward much-needed reforms to the program and toward regional center program permanency, which for the first time in history appears to be a bona fide possibility.

RECENT USCIS DEVELOPMENTS

As the agency in charge of the EB-5 program, USCIS is working hard to keep up with the rapid growth of the industry. In recent years, USCIS has committed substantial time and resources to open a dialogue with EB-5 stakeholders to enact improvements to the program, which ultimately resulted in USCIS's May 30, 2013 Policy Memorandum (PM-602-0083). The memo was published in an effort to clarify the agency's then-current policies for adjudicating EB-5 applications and petitions, and is widely hailed in the industry as the most comprehensive clarification of agency policy to date. The long-term goal of this and other memoranda published by USCIS is to utilize collaboration to promote efficiency, security, predictability, and transparency within the EB-5 program.

To these ends, the agency has also increased public stakeholder meetings.

Implementing Change

As part of these efforts, USCIS opened the Immigrant Investor Program Office in Washington, D.C. in May 2013 and announced that it had committed more than 60 full-time employees, including more than 20 economists and a number of other professionals with experience in areas relevant to the adjudication of EB-5 applications and petitions, including immigration, business, corporate and securities law, and national security.

Changes within USCIS EB-5 program personnel have not just occurred at the staff level. In late 2013, USCIS announced Nicholas Colucci as the new head of the USCIS Immigrant Investor Program Office. Director Colucci has considerable federal government experience, which should help to address concerns and goals recently expressed by members of Congress related to national security, fraud prevention, and the financial integrity of EB-5 capital. Prior to joining USCIS, Colucci served as Associate Director of the Department of Treasury's Financial Crimes Enforcement Network (FinCEN), Analysis and Liaison Division, which is responsible for synthesizing Bank Secrecy Act data with source information to support the needs of domestic law enforcement at government levels, including the intelligence community. This experience should provide an important level of expertise and credibility for addressing the aforementioned concerns.

Proposed Improvements

During his first EB-5 stakeholder meeting, held telephonically on Feb. 26, 2014, Director Colucci introduced three key areas in which he hopes to improve the EB-5 program to increase efficiency, timeliness, consistency, and predictability:

Build the Program's Foundation. Director Colucci wants to build the program's foundation by making personnel and programmatic changes to reduce the backlog, expand the Immigrant Investor Program Office (as discussed above), and increase consistency. By the end of fiscal year 2014, USCIS plans to have grown the program office to 100 individuals, of which most will be dedicated to EB-5 adjudications. New staff members will have to undergo a rigorous, five-week training program and continually attend classes to foster consistency and improve EB-5 program knowledge. Director Colucci will also continue to move forward with the development of a comprehensive policy manual and quality control policy for future guidance, which should help to clarify some of

USCIS's inconsistencies in current rules, regulations, and policies.

Increase Program Performance and Predictability. Director Colucci hopes to increase program performance and predictability, and increase program efficiency, by establishing clear goals and rewarding success.

Improve Customer Service and Transparency. Director Colucci wants the EB-5 program to be more accessible, more responsive, and more informative to EB-5 stakeholders. As a means of keeping program stakeholders more generally informed, USCIS aims to post monthly EB-5 data and statistics on its website, specifically addressing filing times, petitions pending, received, approved or denied, and requests for evidence (RFE) issued. USCIS is currently integrating EB-5 petitions into its Electronic Integration System (ELIS) in an effort to streamline the EB-5 visa application process and reduce the volume of documents submitted with each individual petition. The ELIS is an online, account-based system that is intended to enhance customer service and the quality of the adjudication processes. By creating an ELIS account, immigrant investors can access electronic copies of the documents pertaining to their investment, attest that the documents are true and accurate copies, and supplement their electronic or paper-based I-526 petition with documents stored in the online library.

USCIS reforms aren't strictly limited to the publication of policy memoranda and the incorporation of stakeholder opinion. At the behest of Congressional leaders, and in response to examinations of the EB-5 program by the Office of Inspector General, stakeholder groups and private groups, USCIS announced that it has started drafting revised EB-5 regulations. Proposed regulations will seek to address national security concerns and widely discussed reforms to the EB-5 program. To tap into popular use of social media, USCIS announced its intention to launch a new crowd-sourcing tool called "USCIS Idea Community," an online forum designed to encourage public engagement through social media and to allow stakeholders to post ideas and comments about the EB-5 program.

INTERAGENCY COOPERATION

USCIS has openly sought the input and expertise of other federal agencies to help promote the integrity and near- and long-term goals of the EB-5 program. Most notably, USCIS has sought greater involvement of the US Security and Exchange Commission (SEC) to combat fraud and provide guidance on elements of the EB-5 program more suitably within the SEC's jurisdiction. In October 2013, USCIS and the SEC's Office of Investor Education and Advocacy issued an "investor alert" to warn individual investors about fraudulent investor scams that seek to exploit the EB-5 program. The joint alert, published in multiple languages, provides practical due diligence suggestions and tips for spotting the warning signs of fraud, and is aimed largely at protecting foreign investors who want to immigrate through the EB-5 program.

USCIS and the SEC have also proactively communicated to the EB-5 community their commitment to cultivate EB-5 program integrity. It has been made widely known that the two agencies coordinate on issues at both the programmatic and case-specific levels. In April 2013, USCIS and the SEC held a public event to discuss securities regulations involved in EB-5 offerings for both investors and regional centers. Representatives of the SEC included officials from multiple divisions of the agency. In addition to providing the fundamental point of view that EB-5 investment involves securities—and therefore EB-5 offerings require registration or exemption from the registration requirements under the Securities Act of 1933—the event also emphasized the SEC's anti-fraud enforcement role in the EB-5 program and addressed the use of broker-dealers in EB-5 offerings.

Interagency collaboration by USCIS regarding the EB-5 program has not been limited to interaction with the SEC. USCIS also collaborates with Select USA, an initiative contained within U.S. Department of Commerce's International Trade Administration dedicated to attracting foreign investment and increasing employment in the United States by educating overseas business professionals on services and incentives related to business investment. The objectives of the EB-5 program and Select USA—to foster economic development and job creation within the United States—are remarkably similar, and the Commerce Department has shared its experience with USCIS in recent years. For example, the Commerce Department has served in an advisory role to assist and educate USCIS staff on economic methodologies and prediction of job creation resulting from hotel guest expenditures or retail tenant business activities, and to provide USCIS with useful background data on various industry practices and financial structures. The collaboration has proven beneficial and continues to be supported by proposed legislation from senior congressional leaders, independent audits from the Office of Inspector General, and recommendations by the Brookings Institution that the Department of Commerce increase its role in the EB-5 program and provide more oversight and perhaps even adjudication.

LEGISLATIVE ACTIVITY

The 2013 momentum of immigration reform continues to be a hot topic. Over the course of 2013 and 2014 numerous pieces of legislation on the EB-5 program have been proposed, including as a part of the Senate's immigration reform bill (S. 744).

Among the proposals on the table from this and other legislation is, first and foremost, making the EB-5 regional center program, which has undergone a series of extensions since its inception in 1993, permanent. This would be a tremendous victory for the EB-5 program and job creation in the United States. Additional, important reforms in proposed bills include: an increase in the total number of immigrant visas for the EB-5 program; allowing the recapture of unused immigrant visa allocations from prior fiscal years to use in future years; eliminate per-country quotas for employment-based visas, which would aid investors from China, who account for the largest percentage of EB-5 investors and would most directly be impacted by visa retrogression if the 10,000-visa limit, as predicted, is hit in 2014; and exempt derivative visas for spouses and dependents from the deduction of the current EB-5 visa quota of 10,000—that is, the 10,000-visa number would be determined solely by the number of investors.

Additional provisions still being considered would make further strategic reforms to the EB-5 program, including codification of streamlined processing, expedited processing for pre-approved business plans or exemplar petitions, and provisions empowering the Department of Commerce to provide consultation assistance to determine whether proposed regional centers should be designated, terminated, or subjected to other adjudicative action.

Despite the program improvements, the proposed legislation and amendments also include provisions that stakeholders may find alarming. For example, Congress is entertaining the idea of setting the minimum investment amount to automatically adjust based on changes in the consumer price index. Furthermore, regional centers would be required to conform to additional financial statement reporting requirements and would be subject to financial penalties or termination for non-compliance with such requirements or for activities inconsistent with a regional center's designation. And finally, legislation has been proposed to give unreviewable discretion to the Secretary of the Department of Homeland Security for terminating a regional center. At present, the final form of new EB-5 legislation and its potential for passage remain unknown, but EB-5 stakeholders are optimistic as lines of communication between constituents and Congressional officials remain open and productive.

PREDICTIONS AND ASPIRATIONS OF THE EB-5 PROGRAM

The EB-5 program underwent significant changes in 2013 and it is anticipated that it will experience additional changes in the future. Although opinions vary about the desired direction of EB-5, there a number of issues on which most people agree.

The EB-5 regional center program will sunset in Sept. 2015 without congressional reauthorization. The number one goal for anyone in the EB-5 industry is making the EB-5 regional center program permanent. Making the program permanent is at least on the congressional radar, as it has been included in multiple bills introduced in 2013 and 2014.

Another popular idea is increasing the number of visas available to EB-5 investors. It is anticipated that the EB-5 program will hit its visa cap of 10,000 in 2014, for the first time in the program's history. It is unclear how the resulting "retrogression" will impact the EB-5 program, other than that it will most likely slow down a process already severely backlogged. By increasing the number of visas from 10,000 to 20,000, up to an additional 100,000 US jobs can be created and billions more invested in the US economy.

Should retrogression occur, there will be a cap placed on the number of visas that can be issued to each country. This is important because the vast majority of EB-5 investors come from China. Because of this, one idea gaining in popularity is the removal of per-country cap for EB-5 visas, something the government is already contemplating. However, should that fail to occur, the industry is also exploring opening up the EB-5 market in other countries, including South Korea, India, and Brazil. Obviously, because of foreign banking laws and capital constraints, some countries are more difficult to move into than others. But, the effort to expand the program's popularity is underway.

A practical wish in the EB-5 industry is to see the USCIS backlog decrease. USCIS has taken many positive steps to reduce its backlog of pending I-924, I-526, and I-829 applications, including the hiring of additional qualified staff, the movement toward electronic filing, and the transition of the program to a centralized location in Washington, D.C. Because those efforts are ongoing, however, it is anticipated that the backlog of pending applications and corresponding wait times will increase in 2014, with the anticipated goal of drastically reducing both the backlog and wait times beginning in 2015.

It is important to also examine the possibility that EB-5 will progress in directions that might not be quite as popular. For example, there already exists a noticeable increase in government scrutiny, both by politicians and government agencies. That scrutiny will likely continue as USCIS strengthens its inter-agency relationships with other government entities, including the Department of Commerce, the FBI, and the SEC.

Additionally, the minimum investment amount required by the EB-5 program has been constant since its inception, and there is growing sentiment that it is time to increase the investment amount both for projects located in TEA areas and those outside a TEA area.

Finally, whether it is desired or not, the EB-5 program is gaining popularity in the collective conscience of Americans. Stories regarding EB-5, both positive and negative and with varying degrees of accuracy, are appearing in places like The New York Times and The Wall Street Journal. Because of the publicity generated by a few bad actors in EB-5 and because immigration reform will be a hot-button topic in the upcoming elections, the EB-5 program will remain in the collective conscience for better or worse.

Measuring Success

The benefits to the US economy of the growth of the EB-5 program have been substantial. A recent economic impact study found that the EB-5 program contributed $3.39 billion to the US Gross Domestic Product (GDP) and supported over 42,000 US jobs during fiscal year 2012. These results are substantially greater than those of the identical study done a year ago, which found that the EB-5 program contributed $2.2 billion to the GDP and supported 28,000 jobs in 2011. In addition to their investment capital contributions during 2012, the spending by EB-5 investors also contributed $447 million to federal tax revenues and $265 million to state and local tax revenues. The study, which was conducted by David Kay of IMPLAN Group, LLC and peer-reviewed by Professors Eric Thompson and Hart Hodges of the Association for University Business Economic Research (AUBER), was commissioned by the Association to Invest in the USA (IIUSA).

The EB-5 program is gaining strength and momentum, and is finally starting to realize its potential that lawmakers recognized when they first created the program in 1990.

As the program continues to mature and grow, however, it is imperative that Congress, USCIS (with experienced leadership, qualified personnel, and sufficient allocation of resources), other federal agencies and stakeholders, and well-organized program associations continue to work together to ensure that the growth takes place in a healthy manner that optimizes the program's potential for long-term success. With proper collaboration and planning, and by adopting a clearer set of laws, regulations, and policies, the EB-5 program can continue to flourish while also adequately addressing concerns about national security, fraud prevention, and the financial integrity of the program as a whole. Great strides have already been made to accomplish these goals, and it will be exciting to see how the program continues to grow and mature.

CONTACT INFORMATION
—
PUBLISHER, AUTHORS, AND EDITORS

ALI JAHANGIRI
www.eb5investors.com
Skype: EB5Investors.com
Phone: 18009971228

JEFF CAMPION
Pathways EB5
www.pathwayseb5.com

LINDA HE
Wailian Overseas Consulting Group
www.wailianvisa.com/en

DAVID HIRSON
David Hirson & Partners, LLP
www.hirsonimmigration.com

LINDA LAU
Global Law Group
www.globallawgroup.info

DAWN LURIE
Polsinelli
www.polsinelli.com

JOSEPH MCCARTHY
American Dream Fund
www.adreamfund.com

ELIZABETH PENG
Peng & Weber, PLLC
www.greencardlawyers.com

AL RATTAN
Continental East Development
www.continentaleastdevelopment.com

REID THOMAS
NES Financial
www.nesfinancial.com

JOHN TISHLER
SheppardMullin
www.sheppardmullin.com

KYLE WALKER
Green Card Fund
www.greencardfund.com

CLETUS WEBER
Peng & Weber, PLLC
www.greencardlawyers.com

KEVIN WRIGHT
WrightJohnson
www.wrightjohnsonllc.com

www.ingramcontent.com/pod-product-compliance
Lightning Source LLC
Chambersburg PA
CBHW041304210326
41598CB00005B/19